INTRODUCTION TO
CRIMINAL JUSTICE
RESEARCH METHODS

INTRODUCTION TO CRIMINAL JUSTICE RESEARCH METHODS

By

GENNARO F. VITO, PH.D.

Associate Professor
School of Justice Administration
University of Louisville

EDWARD J. LATESSA, PH.D.

Associate Professor
Department of Criminal Justice
University of Cincinnati

DEBORAH G. WILSON, PH.D.

Associate Professor
School of Justice Administration
University of Louisville

C H A R L E S   C   T H O M A S • P U B L I S H E R
Springfield • Illinois • U.S.A.

Published and Distributed Throughout the World by
CHARLES C THOMAS • PUBLISHER
2600 South First Street
Springfield, Illinois 62794-9265

© *1988 by* CHARLES C THOMAS • PUBLISHER
ISBN 0-398-05490-8 (cloth)
ISBN 0-398-06475-X (paper)
Library of Congress Catalog Card Number: 88-9677

With THOMAS BOOKS *careful attention is given to all details of manufacturing and
design. It is the Publisher's desire to present books that are satisfactory as to their physical
qualities and artistic possibilities and appropriate for their particular use.* THOMAS
BOOKS *will be true to those laws of quality that assure a good name and good will.*

Printed in the United States of America
Q-R-3

Library of Congress Cataloging in Publication Data

Vito, Gennaro F.
  Introduction to criminal justice research methods/
by Gennaro F. Vito, Edward J. Latessa, Deborah G.
Wilson.
        p.   cm.
  Bibliography: p.
  Includes index.
  ISBN 0-398-05490-8. — ISBN 0-398-06475-X (pbk.)
  1. Criminal justice, Administration of — Re-
search — Methodology. I. Latessa, Edward J. II.
Wilson, Deborah G. III. Title.
HV7419.5.V58 1988
364′.072 — dc19   88-9677
                                                        CIP

We dedicate this book to:
Anthony Vito
Amy and Jennifer Latessa
James Wilson

INTRODUCTION

Introduction to Criminal Justice Research Methods is a text designed for criminal justice and criminology students in their second or third year of study. It is based upon our collective experience as instructors in criminal justice programs and as researchers. It is designed to guide students through the research process. Our hope is that our elementary definitions and examples will serve students well as they attempt to understand research reports or, hopefully, to conduct their own research. The text provides a solid foundation for students to follow.

Each of the authors brought specific areas of expertise to this effort. We are familiar with the research process and have worked together on several published studies. The text was a collaborative effort. Vito had primary responsibility for Chapters 1, 4, 6, and 10; Latessa for 2, 7, 8, and 11; and Wilson for 3, 5, and 9.

We express special thanks to the Academic and Professional Development Service of the University of Louisville for their efficient and tireless editing and re-editing of several versions of the manuscript and to Payne Thomas of Charles C Thomas, Publisher for his patience.

CONTENTS

INTRODUCTION TO
CRIMINAL JUSTICE
RESEARCH METHODS

CHAPTER ONE

THE PURPOSE OF
CRIMINAL JUSTICE RESEARCH

T HIS TEXT is designed as an introduction to research methods in criminal justice. We attempt to provide an overview of the basic tools available to conduct and comprehend research reports. These tools are useful and can provide students with worthwhile and relevant abilities. The criminal justice professional must be able to comprehend and implement policy based upon valid information. It is necessary to have the ability to read and comprehend research reports and to make some reasoned judgment about the conclusions which are drawn.

The importance of research in criminal justice operations cannot be overemphasized. For example, Brown[1] has stated that:

> Research methodology is the tool by which virtually all knowledge concerning crime and the administration of justice is derived. It is a multi-faceted tool, the study of which should not be limited to research classes alone, both because it cannot be adequately digested in that limited exposure and because the information conveyed in substantive classes cannot be properly assessed without giving consideration to the process by which that "knowledge" was generated.

Research skills are being recognized as prerequisites for employment in some sectors of the criminal justice system. Kratcoski[4] writes that, in corrections, the job opportunities which require the use of research design skills, evaluation procedures and statistics are increasing. Research skills are neither mundane nor are they limited to the academic world. The criminal justice professional must be able to both comprehend and produce sound research reports.

Naturally, the information contained in research reports cannot and must not be accepted on the basis of faith alone. The criminal justice

3

professional must be able to ascertain the validity of research information in accordance with such methodological issues as the manner in which the study was done or how the research sample was selected and so forth. In fact, the student of research methods should not be intimidated. You will discover that many of the concepts which we will study are familiar to you right now — it is just that the terminology of research is unknown and strange to you.

BASIC CHARACTERISTICS
OF THE SCIENTIFIC METHOD

Research methodology can be viewed as techniques for finding out what has taken place. Essentially, the research method is a procedure (or a blueprint) for carrying out the inquiry. It is typically thorough, logically outlining the procedures of research design, methods of data collection (or observation), measurement of key variables and even the statistical analysis (where appropriate) to be followed.

Often, the research begins with the rather simple process of identifying a problem and determining how to conduct research in this area. For example, a police captain in charge of burglary prevention program could develop the following objective: "The burglary prevention program will reduce the number of burglaries committed in this area." How could this "problem" be reduced to a researchable level? First, it will be necessary to determine how this objective will be measured. What do we mean by burglaries? We may decide upon "burglaries reported to the police" as the **operational definition** of the variable "burglaries." The operational definition of a variable simply refers to the manner in which the variable was measured. Of course, it will also be necessary to determine where the data will be collected, how it will be collected and when it will be collected. These are some of the basic issues of research methodology which will be dealt with in this text.

Like all social sciences, criminal justice research is derived from the basic principles of the scientific method. For example, the hallmarks of the scientific method include both **induction** and **deduction**. Each method relates to the manner in which theory is utilized as a part of the research process. Induction begins with observations (based upon the data collected) and the researcher then develops generalizations to explain the relationships observed. The inductive method develops theory on the basis of research observations. The deductive method takes the opposite approach; applying theory to a particular case. What both methods have in common is absolute faith in reason and the belief that the world operates according to certain laws which can be ascertained through careful study and the collection of empirical evidence. These "laws" will be carefully developed over time as researchers examining the same phenomenon using similar methods (**replication**) to verify the findings of previous studies.

Accordingly, the basic task of research methodology is "error control." As we proceed through this text, you will see that many of the procedures which are established as a part of the research design are actually attempts to isolate and protect the research findings from those sources which could call the results into question. Naturally, there are some forces which are totally beyond the control of the researcher. The task here is to take care of the matters which we can control so that the outcome of the research is not further confounded.

Hypothesis testing is another basic aspect of the scientific method. A **hypothesis** is typically defined as a statement about the nature of things (in this case crime and criminal behavior) which is derived from a theory. For example, consider the following statement:

> If the "Use a Gun, Go to Prison" law is adopted, the number of crimes committed with firearms will decrease.

Where does such an hypothesis come from? In criminological theory, deterrence theory tells us that crime is the result of action freely taken by an individual after a careful assessment of the potential benefits of committing the crime in comparison to its potential costs.[6] Theoretically, the passage of such a law would enter into the calculations made by the offender. The costs of going to prison may outweigh the benefits of the crime. Following the passage of such a law, the criminal justice researcher could develop a research designed which would test not only the impact of the law, but the validity of deterrence theory. In this fashion, hypothesis testing often serves as the "launching pad" for the research design.

THE MYTH OF THE SCIENTIFIC METHOD

Now that these "canons" of the scientific method have been summarized, let us consider another view. Kaplan[3] has written that the scientific method to which all good scientists adhere is actually a reconstruction. Few research projects actually follow this idealized description, especially the social sciences where research is seldom performed under controlled laboratory conditions. Here Kaplan uses the analogy of the "drunkard's search":

> There is a story of a drunkard searching under a street lamp for his house key, which he had dropped some distance away. Asked why he didn't look where he had dropped it, he replied, "It's lighter here!"

In other words, blind adherence to the scientific method does not insure accuracy; yet researchers may feel compelled to report their findings as if they had followed the scientific method to the letter. In fact, from the student's point of view, we would all be far better off if researchers would describe their actual research procedures, warts and all, for instructional purposes. Researchers must identify the limitations of their methodology and describe the steps taken to insure the validity of the research findings. We shall see the description of research procedures is but one of several ethical questions faced by researchers.

ISSUES AND TRADITIONS IN CRIMINAL JUSTICE RESEARCH

Researchers in criminal justice are concerned with the study of criminal behavior and the policies and programs which are developed to deal with this social problem. Naturally, they are committed to the use of criminology as a theoretical base. In this section, we shall review the basic premises of criminological theory and their contribution to and effect upon research methodology.

The Classical School

As previously introduced, the Classical School of Criminology is based upon deterrence theory and a rational, economic model of human behavior. There are two basic premises of deterrence theory: (1) **General deterrence** in which the criminal is punished as an example to others who may contemplate committing a crime and (2) **Specific deterrence** where the offender is punished in order to deter any future crimes undertaken by this individual. As advocated by Beccaria and Bentham, classical theory provided a definite causal explanation of criminal behavior based upon rationalism and free will. In order to deter crime, it was necessary to establish laws which would result in punishments which would outweigh the potential benefits of crime.

Yet, the Classical School had a "due process" aspect as well. When Beccaria wrote that laws should be known, he was not simply speaking to the rational offender but was also protesting a penal system which often reflected the whims of the ruler. The legal code should be just, not arbitrary, in order to maximize the deterrent effect of punishment.

The Classical School has had a dramatic impact upon criminal justice research. Efforts to study the effectiveness of crime control programs, from citizen's crime watch (block watch) programs to the execution of convicted murderers, originate in this school.

Naturally, there are a number of problems associated with deterrence theory research. First of all, how do we know how many potential offenders there are in the general population? How can we estimate how many persons know the penalty for a particular crime? How do we know how many persons are actually deterred as a result of a law or program? After all, deterred persons do not call the police station to report that they were thinking about committing a certain crime but the laws of the state caused them to change their mind. Finally, researchers lack the ability to manipulate deterrents in order to measure their effectiveness. We cannot remove or eliminate a certain law for a period of time and then put it back into place. Nevertheless, deterrence theory has been thoroughly researched and will continue to serve as a focal point as we search for effective and just methods of crime control.

The Positivist School

Perhaps more than the Classical School, the Positivist School of criminology is related to the research tradition of the natural sciences. It is concerned with the development and construction of general laws which can be used to explain and predict criminal behavior.[6] Founded by Lombroso, the Positivist School was concerned with the determination of the causes of crime in the hope that they would lead to the effective treatment of the offender. The focus of study was the individual criminal (in Lombroso's case, prisoners) to determine the attributes related to criminal behavior. Therefore, the Positivist School rests upon a "correctional perspective"[5]: once the causes of crime are identified, something can be done to reduce or eliminate it.

Of course, Lombroso's analysis was based upon the biological studies of Darwin and emphasized the determination of physical attributes associated with crime. Poveda and Schaeffer[5] have stated that Lombrosian theory views crime as a problem of "defective individuals":

> Crime can be controlled through a criminal justice system that appre-
> hends, adjudicates and rehabilitates the individual offender. The em-
> phasis upon treatment overshadows any perceived need for any
> structural changes in society.

Yet, the Positivist tradition is not limited to the biological approach to crime. Typical studies using this approach are concerned with such topics as: the comparison of delinquents to nondelinquents, the evaluation of treatment methods, the prediction of crime and delinquency and probation and parole success.

Clearly, the Positivist School did introduce the use of the scientific method to criminology. Lombroso was one of the first (Queletet and Guerry were the others) to utilize direct measurement and statistical analysis of individuals to study criminality. His studies were thus " 'objective' in method, often statistical" and " 'positive' in the sense of deterministic"; such that the real basis of positivism in criminology is a conception of multiple factor causation, the factors being natural to man and his world, some biological and others environmental."[5]

Of course, the Positivist School is not without its problems. Although Lombroso made the careful attempt to measure the biological attributes of criminals (prisoners) and then compare them to noncriminals (soldiers—as a control group), the basic flaw in this comparison has been with criminology ever since. The "Lombrosian fallacy" is the acceptance of the state or legal definition of crime as a starting point. Do prisoners constitute a true and accurate sample of the actual population of criminals? Or do they simply represent a selective sample of those individuals who have been apprehended and convicted? The use of adjudicated delinquents or convicted prisoners as the research sample reflects this basic problem. Yet, on the other hand, where does one go to find a sample of lawbreakers? The problem is that the use of prisoners as a research sample ignores the fact that the criminal justice system itself is a very selective process and that any patterns observed as a result of the research may be the result of that process, not a true difference which exists in the criminal population.

In fact, this type of research may promote a distorted view of crime patterns. For example, white collar criminals seldom end up in prison and the poor and minority populations are traditionally overrepresented in the prison population. Research in the Positivist tradition can lead to a "kinds of people" interpretation of criminality; that crime is largely a product of individuals who are somehow different from the "normal" citizenry. This type of research fails to question the equity of the criminal justice process and to critically examine the sources of bias in the system. Thus, the Positivist School emphasizes the prediction and control of crime and overlooks the social process of law enforcement.

The Interactionist School

In contrast, the Interactionist School concentrates upon the manner in which laws are made and enforced and critically examines the criminal justice process. Actually, the Interactionist approach is the combination of several criminological theories which share this common theme or purpose (i.e., the "Chicago School" of criminology, Labelling theory, Conflict theory, Anomie theory, Marxist criminology). The Interactionist tradition views crime from the perspective of the criminal or the actor (different functionaries in the criminal justice system).

It often uses Weber's concept of **verstehen**: empathetic understanding of the individual (see Chapter Eight). The legal definition of crime is viewed as a process which can be used against certain elements of society. Unlike the view of the Positivist School, the legal definition of crime is not accepted as a legitimate starting point for the research. The ability of the criminal law to be exercised in a manner which promotes the interests of the dominant classes in society is recognized. Thus, the Interactionist School focuses upon such topics as: the creation of legal norms, the manner in which crime functions to maintain social solidarity, the interrelationship between crime and the criminal justice system, and the development of criminal careers. Unlike the Classical and Positivist Schools, the Interactionist tradition utilizes both quantitative and qualitative methodologies to study crime.

The most telling criticism of the Interactionist School is that it provides a "romanticized view of powerless deviants" and ignores the fact that crime is not completely determined by the social process. Certain behaviors (i.e., murder) would never be accepted by society although it is possible (and some would say probable) that not all murderers will be treated in the same manner in the criminal justice system. The critical edge provided by this school of criminology, while substantial, must be tempered by objectivity.

Criminology as an Applied Social Science

Gilsinian[2] has summarized the "common threads" of these schools of criminology in the following manner:

1. **Tendency Toward Combinations:** People tend to combine things. An undesirable result (crime) is viewed as caused by a pathological condition.
2. **Determinism:** Given a certain pre-existing condition, crime will almost inevitably result.
3. **Rationalism:** The belief in the essentially orderly, understandable nature of human society. The discovery of the "laws" of criminality could lead to control of the crime problem.

We add another attribute to this list. Criminology is not simply aimed at theory construction. Every school seeks to improve the social condition and do something about crime. The Classical School emphasized deterrence for the purpose of crime prevention and crime control (i.e., capital punishment, mandatory sentencing, incapacitation of career criminals). The Positivist School provided a basis for the Medical Model (rehabilitation) of corrections. The Interactionist School promoted the reform of laws (decriminalization: i.e., "status" offenses for juveniles) or even the restructuring of the social order (Marxist) and the critical examination of the discretionary powers of the criminal justice system. Theory feeds research and criminal justice research utilizes this theoretical base to analyze the causes of crime, the manner in which the system operates, and the evaluation of programs which the system offers.

CONCLUSION

This overview of basic research principles and theoretical concepts provides an overview for the body of this text. Research has an important place in the criminal justice system. The information provided by research reports can provide a basis for reform and improvement. This information must be provided in an accurate manner with reliable results.

KEY TERMS

Classical School
Deduction
Determinism
General Deterrence
Hypothesis

Induction
Interactionist School
Operational Definition
Positivist School
Rationalism
Replication
Specific Deterrence
verstehen

REFERENCES

1. Brown, Stephen E.: Research methods and criminal justice curricula: Surmounting the obstacles. *Criminal Justice Review,* 7: 11-16.
2. Gilsinian, James F.: *Doing Justice.* Englewood Cliffs, Prentice Hall, 1982.
3. Kaplan, Abraham: *The Conduct of Inquiry.* Scranton, Chandler, 1964.
4. Kratcoski, Peter C.: Career opportunities in the corrections field. *Journal of Applied Sociology* 2: 25-31.
5. Poveda, Tony G. and Schaffer, Edward: Positivism and interactionism: Two traditions of research in criminology. In Viano, E. (Ed.). *Criminal Justice Research.* Lexington, 1975.
6. Vold, George B. and Bernard, Thomas J.: *Theoretical Criminology.* New York, Oxford University Press, 1979.

CHAPTER TWO

BASIC STATISTICS

MOST UNDERGRADUATE students in criminal justice have an inherent fear of statistics. Yet, statistical information plays a critical role in the criminal justice system. Criminal justice officials and researchers routinely measure crime rates, clearance rates, patterns of criminal activity, recidivism rates and every other conceivable aspect of crime. Since it is not possible to cover all there is to know about statistics in one chapter, we will treat this chapter as an introduction. We will examine only basic statistical concepts and some of the more common statistical tests used in criminal justice research.

PURPOSE OF STATISTICS

Statistics do not replace decision-making, nor do they directly solve problems or answer questions. Rather, statistics are a set of tools which can be used to help make decisions on the basis of limited and variable information. The answer to the question, "What statistic should be used in a given situation?" will depend on answering two questions:

The first question is: What job are you trying to accomplish?

Basically, there are three possible answers to this question:

1. To describe the summary characteristics of a set of scores.
2. To estimate the characteristics of a population with data from a sample of that population.
3. To look for a relationship between two or more variables.

The second question is:

What is the level of measurement of the variables under study? (A variable is a set of mutually exclusive attributes, such as age, gender, marital status, and so forth.)

Before we can address the first question, it is necessary to examine the four levels of measurement.

LEVELS OF MEASUREMENT

Measuring a variable involves the identification of the indicators or attributes of the variable. For example, the indicators of the variable gender are male and female. This variable is discrete, that is, it has a set number of values, in this case two. Other variables, such as prior number of arrests, are thought of as continuous. This implies that the variable is theoretically infinite.

We observe variables at one of four levels: nominal, ordinal, interval, or ratio. As we shall see later, the level of measurement is a critical factor in determining the appropriate statistical test to use.

Nominal Level

The only assumption with a nominal variable is that the score categories of the index **differ** from each other. For example, if Joe is arrested in the Midwest, and Harry is arrested in the West, we may draw one inference: Joe and Harry were arrested in different regions of the country. We cannot arrange regions in any order, or calculate any distance. Many demographic variables are measured on a nominal scale including gender, race, and marital status.

Ordinal Level

A variable measured at the ordinal level assumes that the score categories differ from each other, and that there is a more than or less than relationship among the categories. In other words, the categories of the variable may be arranged in order of magnitude. For example, "Do you believe we can rehabilitate criminals?"

    A. In all cases
    B. Occasionally
    C. Seldom
    D. Never

There is an order among the categories, but the distances are not quantitatively measurable. An easy way to remember this scale is to equate the word order with ordinal. Remember, you can order the items, but you cannot measure exact distance.

Interval Level

An interval scale is a quantitative scale. It assumes that the score categories are different, that there is an order among the categories, and that there is a quantitative, standard unit of measure. With an interval scale you can tell **how many** units one score is more or less than another. An example of an interval scale is "time." For example, if a robbery is reported at 9:00 P.M. and a rape is reported at 11:00 P.M.

1. The crimes were reported at different times.
2. The rape was reported later than the robbery.
3. The rape was reported two hours later than the robbery.
4. We cannot say that the rape is $1/12$ greater than the robbery, because time does not have an absolute zero point.

Ratio Level

A ratio level of measurement is the highest level obtainable. It assumes all of the above, plus that the variable has a **known zero score point.** When you have a zero point, you can state that score X is so many units times score Y. If, for example, we examined the number of prior felony convictions for Harry and Joe:

Joe has six felony convictions and Harry has three. We can then say:

1. Joe and Harry have a different number of felony convictions.
2. Joe has more felony convictions than Harry.
3. Joe has three more felony convictions than Harry.
4. Joe has twice as many felony convictions than Harry. The ratio is two to one.

Since zero felony convictions are possible, we have a ratio scale. The zero anchors the scale and allows the researcher to form ratios.

SCALES AND THEIR PROPERTIES

Properties	Nominal	Ordinal	Interval	Ratio
Classification	+	+	+	+
Ordering	–	+	+	+
Distances	–	–	+	+
Zero Point	–	–	–	+

Levels of measurement are a very important concept, since various statistics require various levels of measurement. We will examine how this works more closely when we calculate some statistical tests later in the chapter.

FREQUENCY DISTRIBUTION

Data can be displayed graphically in a number of ways. The first step in any analysis is to develop a frequency distribution. This is done so that the researcher can examine the range and frequency of the data. For example: Arrest Data

X (Score)	*f (Frequency)*	*fX*
24	1	24
22	1	22
21	1	21
18	2	36
15	3	45
12	4	48
9	1	9
3	5	15
2	8	16
	N = 26	Σfx − 236

This particular distribution indicates that a total of 26 persons had been arrested between two and 24 times. Eight persons were arrested twice, five were arrested three times, and so forth. All together, they accounted for a total of 236 arrests.

DESCRIPTIVE STATISTICS

Getting back to the first question, "What are you trying to accomplish?" our first possibility is to describe the summary set of characteristics of a set of scores. The statistics used to accomplish this task are generally referred to as descriptive statistics.

Descriptive statistics are techniques used to organize and make data understandable. They enable the researcher to describe a sample, and to deal with great quantities of data and to arrange it into a more understandable form. Essentially, they represent a set of techniques for "number crunching."

Perhaps the most common descriptive statistics are the measure of central tendency — the mode, the median and the mean.

Mode

The mode is the **score** which occurs more frequently than any other in a distribution:

	Offense (x)	f
	Murder	10
	Robbery	30
Mode ⟶	Burglary	60

The mode in this example is burglary, since it occurred more frequently (60) than murder or robbery. In the next example we see that a distribution can have more than one mode.

Status (x)	f	
Probation	25	
Parole	15	Mode?
Prison	10	
Jail	25	

In this situation, the distribution is said to be bi-modal. We have 25 people on probation and in jail. The mode can be found at any level of measurement. If there are more than two scores that are the same the distribution is said to be multi-modal.

Median

The second measure of central tendency is the median. It is the point at which 50 percent of the scores lie above and 50 percent lie below. It is the middle, or midpoint of a distribution.

x			x	
95 } 94 }	2 cases		10 } 9 }	2 cases
92	Median	or	7 } 6 }	2 cases
31 } 8 }	2 cases			

(Median = 8)

In our first example, the median is determined by simply counting the number of cases and selecting the one in the middle. When the number of cases are even, as in the second example, you simply add and divide the two middle numbers by 2. So here we add 9 + 7 and divide by 2 which equals 8.

The median divides the distribution into two equal parts. It is the point above and below which 50 percent of the scores lies, the "positional average." Each distribution has one and only one median. It requires an ordinal level of measurement or higher, and it is very stable, that is, it is least affected by extreme scores. The very extreme scores can occur at either end of a distribution but have little or no effect on the median.

Mean

The final measure of central tendency we will examine is the mean ($\overline{X}$). The arithmetic mean is the measure of central tendency for interval and ratio level data. It is the average of the score values of all the cases in the distribution. Because it utilizes all the scores in the distribution it is the most useful and powerful measure of central tendency.

$$\text{Mean} = \frac{\Sigma X}{N} \text{ or } \frac{\Sigma fx}{N}$$

For example:

$$\underline{X}$$
$$5$$
$$4$$
$$3$$
$$2$$
$$\underline{1}$$
$$N = 15$$

$$\overline{X} = \frac{15}{5} = 3$$

or,

x	f	xf
10	1	10
8	2	16
5	5	25
3	7	21
1	10	10
	$N = 25$	$\Sigma fX = 82$

$$\text{Mean} = \frac{\Sigma fx}{N} = \frac{82}{25} = 3.28$$

The mean is very important since it is open to statistical manipulation and comparison. The mean **norms** the sum by translating it into an element amount, a measure of comparability. Unlike the median, the mean is extremely sensitive to extreme scores. In fact, a change in any score value will change the mean, and each distribution has one and only one mean. The mean can only be calculated when the data is interval or ratio level. There is no average for nominal or ordinal level data, since they only serve to classify or order categories.

Descriptive statistics are important because they give a clearer picture of the important characteristics of a set of numbers. They help to describe a set of summary characteristics about a distribution, and thus serve as the beginning point for most statistical analysis.

MEASURES OF VARIABILITY

Now that we have reviewed some descriptive statistics, you should now realize that variation is the foundation of all statistics. After all, if all the values in a given set were identical, then any single score would represent all scores, and any statistic would be meaningless. Thus, the amount of dispersion in the data is highly relevant to measurement of variation, usually considered either:

1. Measurements of range that include all or a specified percentage of items.
2. Averages based upon deviation of the variates from a selected value, usually the mean.

The spread in a set of numbers is important. Often, by combining the information contained in the measures of central tendency and dispersion, the distribution can be more accurately described.

Although there are a number of measurements of variation such as the range, average deviation and semi-interquartile range, we shall only consider the two most important, the variance and the standard deviation.

Variance

The variance is the mean of the sum of all squared deviations from the mean of any distribution of scores. It is an important statistic since it summarizes the amount of dispersion or variance between scores around the mean. The steps to calculate the variance are as follows:

1. Find the mean of the distribution.
2. Find the deviation from the mean $(x = X - \overline{X})$ for each score.
3. Square each x to obtain x^2.
4. Find the mean of the squared deviations. This gives you the average squared deviation from the mean or the variance.
5. $S'^2 = \dfrac{\Sigma fx^2}{N}$

Standard Deviation

The standard deviation is the square root of the variance. It is the single number which is representative of the deviations from the mean found in that distribution. A standard deviation tells you what kind of deviation from the mean is typical of a given population. For most populations you encounter, about two-thirds of all the numbers in the population are within one standard deviation of the mean.

Example: Age of Saturday Night Speeders

Age (X)	f	fX	X (x − $\overline{X}$)	x^2	fx^2
39	1	39	15.3	234.1	234.1
35	4	140	11.3	127.7	510.8
30	3	90	6.3	39.7	119.1
27	7	189	3.3	10.9	76.3
25	5	125	1.3	1.7	8.5
21	9	189	− 2.7	7.3	65.7
18	15	270	− 5.7	32.5	487.5
	N = 44	1042			1502.0

$$\overline{X} = \frac{\Sigma fX}{N} = \frac{1042}{44} = 23.7 \qquad S'^2 = \frac{\Sigma fx^2}{N} = \frac{1502}{44} \qquad S' = \sqrt{S'^2} = \sqrt{34.1}$$

$$S'^2 = 34.1 \qquad\qquad S' = 5.8$$

So, for this particular distribution we have a variance of 34.1 and a standard deviation of 5.8.

THE NORMAL DISTRIBUTION

Statistics and parameters are two terms that we will encounter and it is important that you not become confused about their meaning. A parameter is a measurement of an entire population, while a statistic is a measurement of a sample.

A normal curve refers to a certain type of distribution of scores. The word "normal" refers to the type of curve and distribution having certain properties. In essence, it involves only two summarizing measures, the mean and the standard deviation. Thus, the exact form of the normal curve will be known if we are given the values of both the mean and the standard deviation.

GRAPH 1

Normal Distribution

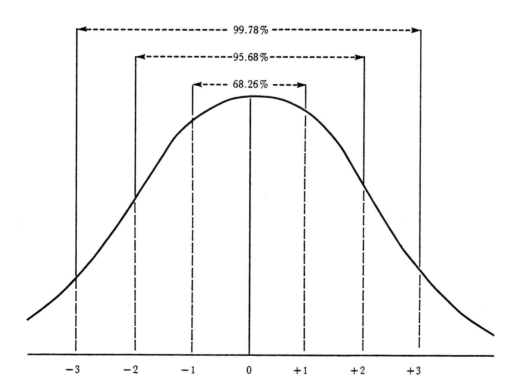

Not all symmetrical bell shaped curves are normal. They can differ with respect to their peakedness, due to differences in their standard deviation. One of the more desirable properties of the normal curve is that it can be used to define a series of constant attributes. The total area under the normal curve can represent the total number of units in a population. Due to this property, it is possible to determine the proportion of frequencies contained between any two scores along the x-axis by determining the area under the curve between the two scores. The normal curve can thus serve as an instrument to standardize scores taken from different distributions. It has a general comparative function.

A normal curve is always symmetrical and bell-shaped. It is asymptotic, which means that the ends of the distribution extend toward infinity, approaching the horizontal axis but never quite touching it. The range of the normal distribution is theoretically infinite. The mean, median, and mode all occur at the same point, dividing the distribution into two equal parts. As displayed above, the distance in standard deviation units may be converted into a percentage of the total area. Because of its symmetry, approximately two-thirds (68.26%) of the cases lie in the interval extending plus or minus one standard deviation unit above and below the mean. Similarly, approximately 95 percent of the cases fall within plus or minus two standard deviation units on either side of the mean. Finally, the mean of the normal distribution is always defined as zero and the standard deviation is always equal to one. This provides a common standard to compare scores taken from different distribution. If, as an example, we plotted the crime rates for each city the distribution would approximate the normal curve. This means that the crime rates for various areas would be distributed around the mean in a known manner. About 68 percent of all the scores would fall within plus or minus one standard deviation around the mean, and about 95 percent within plus or minus two standard deviations. We would then be able to compare a sample of selected cities' crime rates using the normal distribution as a basis for our decision regarding our hypothesis.

HYPOTHESIS TESTING

Statistical Inference consists of two types:

1. Estimation. This is the process of statistically "guessing" the location of the population mean on the basis of a sample mean. We began with a sample mean and then, within a specified degree of confidence

made an estimate of an interval which would contain the population mean. In this manner, an interval estimate begins with sample data and ends with a range of values which probably includes the population mean.

2. Hypothesis Testing. Hypothesis testing begins with a hypothesis about the parameter and then uses the sample data to test the accuracy of the hypothesis. Thus, hypothesis testing begins with an assumption about population value and hypothesis on the basis of the sample data.

Types of Hypotheses

Research hypotheses are derived from theories held by the researcher or derived from the other sources. They generally state a specified relation between two or more variables. Or they are tentatively held suppositions about what is, how things change, or how events are interrelated.

A statistical hypothesis is a statement, assertion or claim about the nature of a population. So the research hypothesis generally must be stated in statistical form in order to be tested. One form of statistical hypothesis is the Null Hypothesis — the hypothesis of no difference (designated as H_0). The H_0 is formulated with the full expectation that it will be rejected or "nullified." Usually, the research hypothesis is supported when it is nullified and is unsupported when we fail to nullify it. Therefore, the null hypothesis is tested against the research (or alternative) hypothesis (H_1).

H_0: There is no difference in the number of accidents caused by drunken driving before and after the passage of a new "tough" DUI law.

H_1: The number of accidents attributable to drunken drivers decreased following the passage of the new law.

A test of a statistical hypothesis is a rule or procedure that leads to a decision to accept or to reject the hypothesis when the experimental sample values are obtained. These rules are called decision rules and they help us to decide how to judge the observations contained in the data. Decision rules involve specifying the sampling distribution of a statistic, the level of significance, and the region of rejection in the sampling distribution. A sampling distribution of a statistic is the distribution of all possible values that any statistic may assume, based upon random sampling of a specified size from a specified universe. In turn, this distribution specifies probabilities associated with the occurrence of any statistical value. Thus, decision rules involve the specification of identification of a sampling distribution which will help in the support or rejection of statistical hypotheses.

Testing the Null Hypothesis (H_0)

One important principle of this procedure is that we can never prove the null hypothesis true. This is due to the fact that even if we found or obtained a sample value precisely equal to our hypothesized value, we could still not be positive that H_0 was true. Why? This result could be due to sampling error. By the same token, we can never be absolutely sure that H_0 is false, but the statistical evidence may be more convincing when the null hypothesis can be rejected within a certain range of probability. The level of significance refers to the probability that we are wrong in rejecting H_0. If we hypothesize that there is no difference between two sample means at the .05 level of significance there is a difference at this level, we are saying that 5 times out of 100 we are wrong in rejecting H_0. When testing hypotheses, we have two possibilities regarding H_0.

1. H_0 is true.
2. H_0 is false.

If H_0 is true and we reject it, we have committed a Type I error, α, known as alpha, and referred to as the level of significance. Accept H_0; correct decision probability = $1 - \alpha$. If the H_0 is true and we reject H_0, we have made an incorrect decision probability = α. If the H_0 is false, and we accept it, we have committed a Type II error, or β (beta).

H_0 is true:	Correct decision probability = $1 - \alpha$	Incorrect decision; Type II error; probability = α
H_0 is false: (H_1 is true)	Incorrect decision; Type II error; probability = β	Correct decision probability = $1 - \beta$

A jury trial requires proof beyond reasonable doubt to prove guilt.

H_1: The defendant is guilty.
H_0: The defendant is not guilty.

The prosecution sets out to destroy the null hypothesis. Also, if the accused goes free, it does not mean that he/she is innocent. This example illustrates the aura of probability surrounding H_0.

	Innocent	Guilty
Acquitted	True	Type I error
Convicted	Type I	True

In sum, the decision to reject or not to reject H_0 is based upon the location of the test statistic in is sampling distribution.

Steps of Hypothesis Testing

1. State your research hypothesis.
2. State the null hypothesis.
3. Choose an appropriate statistical test; one for which all required assumptions can be met.
4. Specify a significance level (α) and a sample size (N).
5. Find or assume the sampling distribution of the statistical test under the H_0. This is done in order to make probability statements about certain values associated with the statistic.
6. On the basis of 2, 3, and 4, define the region of rejection.
7. Compute the value of the statistical test, using the data obtained from the sample.
8. Make a decision regarding the null hypothesis and interpret the findings.

NON-PARAMETRIC VS. PARAMETRIC STATISTICS

The parametric tests are the most powerful tests available, and they generally require measurements at the interval or ratio level. You should use them whenever possible. However, parametric tests specify certain conditions about the distribution from which the research sample was drawn:

a. Observations must be independent. The selection of any one case from the population for the sample must not bias the chances of any other case for selection.
b. Observations must be drawn from normally distributed populations.
c. Populations should have equal variances.

d. The data should be at the interval or ratio level of measurement.
e. Additive effects of the above conditions.

Before any confidence can be placed in the probability statement obtained by the use of the parametric test, these conditions should be met. The problem is that many of the measurements taken in the criminal justice field are nominal or ordinal, thus making it necessary to use less powerful tests called non-parametric statistics. A non-parametric statistical test is a test whose model does not specify conditions about the parameters of the population from which the sample was drawn. The disadvantage is that if the assumptions are met, then non-parametric tests tend to waste data. What to do in practice!

1. Meet as many of the assumptions as you can but: Non-parametric statistics allow you to relax these assumptions. This is the major advantage of non-parametric statistics.
2. Or as Siegel[1] argues, by increasing the size of your sample, you can increase the power of non-parametric statistics to equal that of parametric tests.

A non-parametric statistical test is one whose model does not specify the conditions about the parameters of the population from which the sample was drawn. There are four major advantages of non-parametric tests:

1. Probability statements obtained from most non-parametric tests are exact probabilities, regardless of the shape of the population distribution from which the random sample was drawn.
2. Small samples can be used (N = 6 or less). This is impossible with parametric statistics.
3. No assumption is made about homogeneity of variance.
4. Can be used at any level of measurement.

Non-parametric tests provide an alternative when assumptions cannot be met, so you don't have to let assumptions stand in your way. If your hypothesis is important and requires a violation, do it, provided that you are aware that the assumptions are being violated and you know the effects of the violation. Always remember to use the classic probability level (.05), unless you have a strong reason not to. Use as large a sample as possible. Choose the population before you select the sample. Use the simplest statistic which answers the hypothesis (this means of course that you must know precisely what the hypothesis states).

Now, let's examine some of the more common statistical tests used in criminal justice research. The first one we'll look at is called the t-test. This is a parametric statistic based on the t distribution. It is used primarily with small samples, generally less than 30.

T-Test

Often, our research question involves examining the difference between two samples of elements.

a. Are delinquent boys more likely to have learning disabilities?
b. Does one region of the country differ from another with respect to crime rates?

The statistical implication here is that the difference between the two groups is significant. The t-test is essentially determining whether or not the difference between $\bar{X}1$ is significantly different than $\bar{X}2$. Remember, in order to obtain a mean you must have measurements at least interval level.

The type of t-test chosen will depend upon whether or not the two samples are independent or non-independent (related). Related samples occur in the following ways:

1. When both samples have been matched according to some trait, i.e., race or gender.
2. Linked relationship (husbands and wives).
3. Repeated measurements of the same sample (before-after or time series design).

Independent samples are selected in such a way as to permit the assumption that they are unrelated to one another according to any variable.

T-Test for Independent Samples

Let's suppose that we have two types of counties, one urban and one rural, and we compare them with respect to the percentage of persons who feel that crime is a real problem. Note that t does not assume a negative value, so when you calculate a t-test, either position your sample means so that the largest mean is first or simply ignore the sign of your t value.

Urban	*Rural*
N = 33	N = 19
$\bar{X}_1 = 57$	$\bar{X}_2 = 52$
$\Sigma X_1^2 = 56$	$\Sigma X_2^2 = 52$

First we must obtain the "pooled variance":

$$S^2 = \frac{\Sigma X_1^2 + \Sigma X_2^2}{N + N - 2} = \frac{56 + 72}{33 + 19 - 2} = \frac{128}{50} = 2.56$$

This amounts to a "pooling" of the standard errors of each of the means in order that we may more properly evaluate the differences between them. The pooling takes into account the differences in sample sizes and the differences in standard deviations of variance. Next, we calculate the standard error of the difference:

$$^S\overline{X}_1 - \overline{X}_2 = \frac{S^2}{N_1} + \frac{S^2}{N_2} = \frac{2.56}{33} + \frac{2.56}{19} = .46$$

Finally, calculate the t-test.

$$t = \frac{\overline{X}_1 - \overline{X}_2}{^S\overline{X}_1 - \overline{X}_2} = \frac{57 - 52}{.46} = \frac{5}{.46} = 10.86$$

As with most inferential statistics, the t value must be located on a distribution table to determine whether or not it is significant. Most statistic texts have these tables. For this problem, a t value of 1.67 is required for significance at the .05 level. Since our obtained value was higher, our decision would be to reject the null hypothesis and to conclude that people that live in urban areas feel that crime is more of a problem than people that live in rural areas.

T-Test for Related Sample

Suppose a prison counselor wishes to know if his caseload is learning the principles of Reality Therapy. He tests them at the very beginning of the program, and then again six months later at the close of the treatment.

Individual	Test #1	Test #2	D	D^2
A	63	68	5	25
B	41	49	8	64
C	54	53	− 1	1
D	71	75	4	16
E	39	49	10	100
F	44	41	− 3	9
G	67	75	8	64
H	56	58	2	4
I	61	55	− 6	36
N = 9	ΣX_1 496	ΣX_2 523	ΣD 27	ΣD^2 319

Here, you would subtract the score on test #1 from the score on test #2 because, if the treatment is effective and a prisoner did learn the principles of reality therapy, his score on the second test (after the treatment) should be higher than his score on the first test (before the treatment).

First compute the mean for each group:

$$\overline{X}_1 = \frac{\Sigma X_1}{N} = \frac{496}{9} = 55.11 \qquad\qquad \overline{X}_2 = \frac{\Sigma X_2}{N} = \frac{523}{9} = 58.11$$

Now compute the population variance of difference scores:

$$S_D^2 \quad \frac{N\Sigma D^2 - (\Sigma D)^2}{N(N-1)} = \frac{9(319) - (27)^2}{9(8)} = \frac{2142}{72} = 29.75$$

Next compute the estimation of the Population Standard Error of the Mean Difference Scores:

$$S_{\overline{D}} = \sqrt{\frac{S_D^2}{N}} = \sqrt{\frac{29.75}{9}} = \sqrt{3.305} = 1.82$$

Finally, calculate the t test:

$$t = \frac{\overline{X}_1 - \overline{X}_2}{S_{\overline{D}}} = \frac{55.11 - 58.11}{1.82} = \frac{3}{1.82} = 1.65$$

For this example, a t value of 1.96 would be required at the .05 level. Since we did not obtain this value, our decision would be to accept the null hypothesis and conclude that the prisoners had not learned the principles of Reality Therapy.

In interpreting the t-test you should remember that the magnitude of the t is not necessarily indicative of the magnitude of the difference between means. A statistically significant difference does not necessarily indicate a cause and effect relationship, and the statistical inference drawn should be limited to the population sampled.

Chi-Square

One of the most widely used statistical tests is chi-square. This non-parametric statistic tells us whether our observations differ significantly from what would be expected by chance. "Chance" is defined in a particular way.

Chi-square is a "goodness of fit" statistic. Goodness of fit refers to a statistical evaluation of the difference between our sample observations and some distribution of observations provided by our hypothesized model of expected values at a given level of significance. It is a test of significance for nominal data. Data should be discrete and expressed in frequencies in the form of a contingency table.

Chi-Square for Two Independent Samples

Often, we are interested in determining whether or not our observations are significantly different from what we would expect according to chance. Suppose we would like to know whether significant differences in social class background exists between prisoners confined for a variety of offenses:

RELATIONSHIP BETWEEN SOCIAL CLASS AND TYPE OF CRIME FOR 200 PRISONERS

	Prisoner Social Class	
Type of Crime	Upper or Middle	Working or Lower
Property	A 75 (57.5)	B 40 (57.5) 115
Personal	C 25 (42.5)	D 60 (42.5) 85
Total	100	100

H_0: There is no difference in the type of crime committed by prisoners of different social class backgrounds.

H_1: Upper Class Prisoners are more likely to be convicted of a property crime.

First, it is necessary to calculate the expected frequency (E) for each cell.

$$E = \frac{(N \text{ row}) (N \text{ column})}{N \text{ Total}}$$

$$\text{Cell A} = \frac{(115) (100)}{200} = 57.5$$

$$\text{Cell B} = \frac{(115) (100)}{200} = 57.5$$

$$\text{Cell C} = \frac{(85) (100)}{200} = 42.5$$

$$\text{Cell C} = \frac{(85) (100)}{200} = 42.5$$

Next, calculate the value of chi-square:

Cell	O	E	($\mid$O-E$\mid$ – .5)	($\mid$O-E$\mid$ – .5)^2	Divided by E
A	75	57.5	17	289	5.03
B	40	57.5	17	289	5.03
C	25	42.5	17	289	6.80
D	60	42.5	17	289	6.80

$$x^2 = 23.66$$

Where: O = Observed frequency
E = Expected frequency
– .5 = Yates's correction for continuity*

*Note: Yates's correction for continuity should only be used when the degrees of freedom = 1 or when one of the expected cell frequencies is less than 10.

Determine if the chi-square value is statistically significant:

In order to calculate the degrees of freedom with two independent samples you subtract one from the number of rows and columns and multiply: (rows – 1) (columns – 1).

For a 2×2 table, a value of 3.84 is required to reject the null hypothesis. Since our obtained value (23.66) was greater, we reject the null hypothesis, and conclude that there was a difference in type of offense and social class background of prisoners. In order to fully interpret the chi-square we must inspect the data, since chi-square does not indicate direction. We can see from these data that upper and middle class prisoners were more likely to have committed property crimes than lower or working class prisoners. This is an important point to remember, since if the exact same numbers were simply reversed we would have obtained the same chi-square value, but our interpretation would have been completely reversed.

Assumptions Behind the Use of Chi-Square

a. The sample of observations must be independent.
b. Data can exist at any level of measurement.
c. But, no cell should have an expected frequency of less than 5.

When chi-square is computed when the expected cell frequencies drop below 5, the resulting value is meaningless.

One of the reasons why chi-square is so popular is the absence of restrictions on its use. The only disadvantage: The smaller the sample, the more distorted the chi-square value is likely to be. Distortion is introduced when any expected frequency is less than 5. The resulting chi-square value becomes an overestimate of the "way things are."

Measures of Association for Nominal and Ordinal Data

Up to this point, we have been interested in whether or not a relationship exists between variables. Two measures of association, the contingency coefficient and the phi coefficient, are often utilized with chi-square to measure the magnitude and nature of a relationship.

Contingency Coefficient

The contingency coefficient (C) is a measure of association for use with nominal level data. It can be used with data which has been divided into more than two categories.

$$C = \sqrt{\frac{x^2}{N + x^2}} \quad C = \sqrt{\frac{23.66}{200 + 23.66}} = \sqrt{.105} = .32$$

Unlike the correlation coefficients, C does not have + or − 1.00 as its lower and upper limits. With an equal number of columns and rows, the upper limit of C is equal to:

$$\sqrt{\frac{(K - 1)}{K}}$$

where K = the number of rows. With an unequal number of columns and rows, the upper limit follows that of the smaller number.

C has no sign, so you must determine the direction and nature of the relationship by inspecting the contingency table. The major advantage of C is that there are no assumptions regarding the population distribution. It can be applied to data which are normal, skewed, continuous, discrete, nominal, ordinal, etc. Remember, if the chi-square value is statistically significant, so is the value of C.

Phi

The Phi coefficient is only used when data are dichotomized. If the data is divided in any other fashion, the use of C is more appropriate.

$$Phi = \sqrt{\frac{x^2}{N}} = \sqrt{\frac{23.66}{200}} = .34$$

Again, if the value of the chi-square is significant, so is the value of Phi.

To evaluate the magnitude of the association, compare the computed Phi with the maximum value of Phi for this type of split. To set the maximum value, make the cell with the lowest frequency equal to zero and then compare this value to your computed phi value. Remember, you should use C if you do not have a 2 × 2 table.

Correlation

Often, the criminal justice researcher wishes to measure the extent to which two or more variables are "related" to each other. In order to answer this question, it is necessary to determine:

1. Whether or not an association exists.
2. The magnitude of strength of the association.
3. The nature of the relationship.

Correlation is a measure of relationship between two variables. It indicates the degree to which two (or more) variables are associated with each other. The numerical value of measures of association, like the Pearson's Correlation Coefficient, range in value from −1.00 to +1.00 (perfect correlation). Note that a correlation of +.65 is the same size as one of −.65. The sign indicates the direction of the relationship, **not** the strength. When two variables are positively related, as one increases, the other increases, or as one decreases the other decreases, i.e., number of handguns in the population, and the number of homicides. When two variables are inversely related, as one increases, the other decreases, or as one decreases, the other increases, i.e., the number of beat patrolmen, amount of crime committed. A value of .00 would indicate the absence of a relationship.

The first step with correlation is to draw a scatter diagram. This permits the research to examine the extent of the relationship between two variables in a preliminary and informal manner. It generally indicates whether or not there is an apparent relationship, and if there is a relationship, it may suggest whether it is linear or non-linear. If the relationship is linear, the scatter diagram will show whether the relationship is positive or negative. Figures A through D in Graph 2 illustrate some of the possible relationships that are possible with correlation. Here we can see a perfect positive relationship in which a straight line runs from the lower left of the scatter diagram to the upper right. With the perfect negative relationship, the points fall along a straight line, running from the upper left corner of the scatter diagram to the lower right corner. We also see examples of a very weak relationship and a curvilinear relationship. The strength is generally gauged by the number of scores which group around some central direction.

GRAPH 2

A. Positive

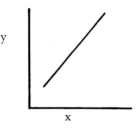

B. Negative

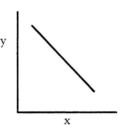

C. No Apparent Correlation

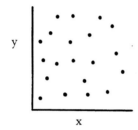

D. Curvilinear

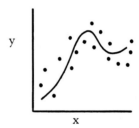

The measure of association that we will examine here is the Pearson's Product Moment Correlation, or R. There are two assumptions which surround its use:

1. The data must be at least interval in nature.
2. The association between the two variables must be linear.

Formula:

$$r = \frac{N\Sigma XY - (\Sigma X)(\Sigma Y)}{\sqrt{N\Sigma X^2 - (\Sigma X)^2 \ N\Sigma Y^2 - (\Sigma Y)^2}}$$

Where: N = number of pairs of values
           ΣXY = the sum of the cross products of the paired scores.

Example: We wish to examine the number of executions in eight states and the number of homicides in these states in the three months following the executions.

X = Executions
Y = Homicides

States	X	Y	XY	X^2	Y^2
1	10	10	100	100	100
2	8	10	80	64	100
3	6	4	24	36	16
4	5	8	40	25	64
5	5	7	35	25	49
6	3	4	12	9	16
7	2	8	16	4	64
8	1	3	3	1	9
N = 8	40	54	310	264	418

GRAPH 3

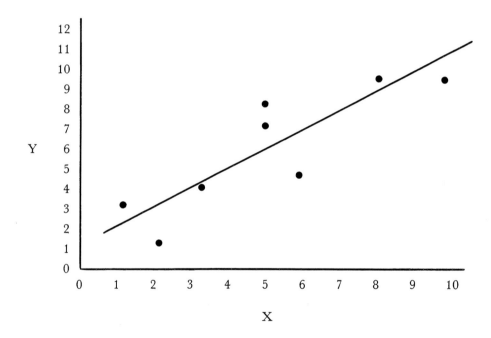

What can we say about the linearity of the relationship between these two variables?

The first step in calculating Pearson's R is to set up the preceding table. Then:

A. Pair the values of X and Y.
B. Sum the values of X, ΣX.

    C. Sum the values of Y, ΣY.

    D. Multiply the two numbers in each pair, then sum the cross products, ΣXY.

    E. Square all values of X, then sum them, ΣX^2.

    F. Square all values of Y, then sum them, ΣY^2.

    G. $N\Sigma XY = (8)\ (310) = 2480$.

    H. $(\Sigma X)\ (\Sigma Y) = (40)\ (54) = 2160$

    I. $N\ XY - (\Sigma X)\ (\Sigma Y) = 2480 - 2160 = 320$

Thus, with steps A through I you have calculated the value of the numerator.

    J. $N\Sigma X^2 = (8)\ (264) = 2112$

    K. $(\Sigma X)^2 = (40)^2 = 1600$

    L. $[N\Sigma X^2 - (\Sigma X)^2] = 2112 - 1600 = 512$

    M. $N\ Y^2 = (8)\ (418) = 3344$

    N. $(\Sigma Y)^2 = (54)^2 = 2916$

    O. $[N\Sigma Y^2 - (\Sigma Y)] = 3344 - 2916 = 428$

    P. Multiply step L $\times$ step O.

    Q. Take the square root $\sqrt{219,136} = 467.8$

How with steps J through Q, you have calculated the value of the denomination of the formula.

$$R = \frac{320}{467.8} = .684$$

Degrees of freedom for R = Number of pairs – 2.

    A value of .7067 is required for significance at the .05 level. Therefore, our decision would be to accept the null hypothesis.

Interpreting Correlation

    Correlation characterizes the existence of a relationship between variables. However, it says nothing about the reasons for the existence of a relationship between variables. It indicates only that two or more variables vary together either positively or negatively. The existence of a correlation between two variables **is not** an unfailing clue to the existence of a cause and effect relationship.

Often, the effect of these variables upon the original relationship is concealed. When this occurs, we have encountered a **spurious** correlation: a correlation in which hidden factors exert an effect on Y which is erroneously credited to X.

In order to interpret R we normally consider the following steps:

Is the obtained R significant or not? Can we reject the null hypothesis of no correlation? If yes, then consider:

a. What is the direction of the relationship, positive or negative?

b. What is the magnitude of the relationship? Unlike the first two steps, gauging of the magnitude of the relationship calls for the subjective judgment of the researcher. Statistical significance only puts the researcher in a position to interpret the magnitude of the correlation, it does not do this for them. The following is a rough guide of how the **magnitude** of R is generally interpreted. It follows for either positive or negative correlation.

< .20	slight, negligible
.20 – .40	low, definite but small
.40 – .70	moderate, substantial
.70 – .90	high, marked
> .90	very high, very dependable

Another important feature of correlation is R^2, the coefficient of determination. R^2 expresses the proportion of the variance of Y "determined" by X, considering X as the independent and Y as the dependent variable. It also helps to interpret the magnitude of the correlation. For example, our R = .684, R^2 = .467. So, 46.7 percent of the variance of Y is "determined" or "explained" by X. Remember, "determined" does not mean "caused by."

CONCLUSION

In this chapter we have attempted to introduce some of the basic concepts and principles of statistical testing, and some of the more common statistical tests available to the criminal justice researcher. Many fine statistics texts can provide more detailed and comprehensive coverage of statistical testing.

The statistical tests presented, such as correlation, chi-square, and t-test are only three of the many inferential statistics that are available to the criminal justice researcher. They illustrate how statistical testing can be used in a criminal justice setting to examine programs, policies, and to test theories.

KEY TERMS

Frequency Distribution
Median
Mode
Mean
Variance
Standard Deviation
Null Hypothesis

STUDY GUIDE

1. What is the purpose of statistics?
2. Name the four levels of measurement and their characteristics.
3. What are the measures of central tendency?
4. What is a normal distribution?
5. What are the steps of hypothesis testing?
6. What are the differences between parametric and non-parametric tests?
7. When is a t-test most appropriate?
8. Describe a situation in which the chi-square would be used.
9. What are measures of association?
10. How is correlation interpreted?

REFERENCE

1. Siegel, Sidney: *Non-Parametric Statistics.* New York, McGraw-Hill, 1956.

CHAPTER THREE

ETHICAL ISSUES IN CRIMINAL JUSTICE RESEARCH

ACCORDING TO *Webster's New Collegiate Dictionary*, ethics are "moral principles or values," "principles of conduct governing an individual or a profession." All research raises certain ethical issues and concerns. While these ethical issues have always been a part of scientific research, it was not until World War II that the importance of these ethical issues became obvious. The inhumane Nazi experimentation on human beings and the research which culminated in the atomic bomb brought the consideration of ethics in scientific research to the forefront of scholarly and public concern. Prior to this time, science was viewed as an objective, value-free process. These two events brought forth evidence that inhumane acts on human beings were performed in the name of science and that the products of scientific research could produce dangerous and harmful devices.[1] These events produced the need for scientists to recognize that their research is not value-free and that they must adhere to a set of guidelines and principles which will uphold moral values.

Ethics are a special consideration in social and behavioral research. This research, like medical research, frequently utilizes human subjects. Serious thought must be given to the treatment of human subjects as well as the researcher's responsibility for the outcome or consequences of his or her work. For example, Longmire states that ". . . among some of the most ethically infamous research there is a strong representation of criminologically based research."[7] While researchers in the area of criminology and criminal justice are confronted with a number of ethical dilemmas common to social or behavioral research, the nature of the subject matter makes ethical issues more acute. Specifically, the subject matter of much of this research is deviant or criminal behavior. Much of the information on deviant or criminal behavior must be acquired from those who are engaging in these types of acts. As a result, issues relating to the treatment of the subject are especially relevant.

ETHICAL PROBLEMS IN RESEARCH

The ethical problems which confront a researcher may be categorized into four areas: (1) potential harm, (2) informed consent, (3) deception, (4) privacy.[1] Problems in these areas are confronted at every phase of the research process. Their resolution requires careful and thoughtful assessments of the value of the research in relation to the potential harm of the research and the rights of individuals.

Potential Harm

Every research project carries with it the potential to be harmful. The harm can be of two types: harm related to the results of the research and harm to the subjects of the research either during or following their participation in the research project.

Researchers value the freedom they are provided in the course of research by both the academic and research tradition. Nonetheless, every research project does not necessarily benefit society. Neither does every research project and its findings carry with it the same potential for abuse, misuse, or misrepresentation. Researchers must be sensitive to these issues. The research topic, findings, and in some instances, the sponsor must be taken into account in determining the potential harm posed by a research project. The cases described below suggest some of the potential harm related to research projects.

> A researcher engages in a study of illicit and illegal behavior among inmates in a correctional facility. The warden of the facility receives a copy of the research findings and uses them to justify a dramatic restriction on the visitation rights of all inmates in the facility. To what extent is the researcher responsible for this use of the research?
>
> A researcher has been asked to conduct a study of the fairness of application of the death penalty by the state's Attorney General. As part of the funding contract, the researcher must agree to have his or her findings reviewed and approved by the Attorney General prior to their release or publication. The Attorney General is involved in a close re-election campaign. The Attorney General's opponent has as one of his

election issues the unfair application of sentences of death in the state. What ethical concerns are involved? What options could researchers with different values take advantage of?

While the harm or potential harm which follows from these examples is not intentional, the researchers must be aware of harmful consequences and use ethical guides as a means of resolving conflicts that may exist between the scholarly and practical rewards of research and the potential harm that might follow from it.

The potential harm resulting from a research project may also involve harm to the subjects. As stated earlier, when the area of interest is deviant or criminal behavior the potential of harm to the subject is increased. Subjects who are engaging in deviant or criminal activities seek to avoid detection. If they are the subject of a research project which discloses these activities there might be harmful consequences for both them and their families. For example, the disclosure of drug abuse among doctors could have serious ramifications for the doctors and their families should their identities be disclosed. Harm may also follow from experimental situations that subjects are placed in during the course of a research project. Subjects may be exposed to mental or psychological stress, undue hardship, or physical harm during their participation in a project. Correctional officers may be placed in extremely stressful situations in order to gauge their reactions. This may have short and long term consequences for these officers as subjects. Harm may also follow from a subject's non-exposure to an experimental condition or treatmet. Individuals may be randomly assigned to detention or pretrial release status to assess the probability of risk involved in pretrial release programs. Those placed in detention would then be experiencing harm because they were not given the opportunity for pretrial release. Finally, harm may follow from being involved in a research project simply because an individual agreed to participate. An inmate who is a sex offender but who has not made his offense known to other inmates may agree to participate in an experimental sex offender treatment program. Through this involvement, his offense becomes known and the other inmates begin to harass him. He has been harmed not by specific experimental conditions but solely by his agreement to participate.

Concern over harm to subjects is based on a number of principles. First, individuals have basic rights. One of these is the right to avoid harmful situations. Secondly, science has as one of its goals to provide knowledge that is of benefit to society. To harm individuals while attempting to provide a benefit to society is inconsistent. The subjects are members of society too. Finally, if science harms individuals in the course of the research process, this may generate a distrust of the scientific enterprise and make research, such as criminological and criminal justice research, which requires human subjects more difficult, if not impossible.

Researchers have different beliefs about the justification of harm to subjects. Some have argued that harm is acceptable if it is necessary to obtain research results and further knowledge development. However, this can lead to serious abuse of the rights of individuals and distrust of the research enterprise. Another position is that harm that is infrequent, rare, or minimal may be justified as long as the subjects are aware of the risks. This too can be problematic. Researchers cannot always predict the probability nor the extent of harm. For example, in an attempt to study the strength of social-situational variables on behaviors, Zimbardo[21] created a simulated prison environment in the basement of a university building. Student subjects were then assigned roles as either guards or prisoners. The project was to run for two weeks but was terminated after six days. The students, who had all been screened to ensure for "normal" subjects, began exhibiting extremely stereotypic role behavior. The guards were verbally and physically abusive to the inmates and seemed to enjoy their power and misuse of power. The prisoners were subjected to the abuse and became subservient and "powerless." The experiment proved too stressful for some prisoners and they had to be released. Could Zimbardo have predicted the extreme behaviors and the consequent harm that resulted from his prison experiment? It is doubtful. Nonetheless, harm resulted and when this occurs, the researcher is responsible for that harm.

Informed Consent

Another problem of research which confronts criminological and criminal justice researchers is the informed consent of subjects. Informed consent means that the subjects participated in the research voluntarily with an adequate knowledge of the risks involved and with the knowledge that they have the option of withdrawing their consent to participate at any point during the course of the research.

Informed consent is important to the research process. Basic common sense also tells us that the best protector of the interests of a person is the individual him or herself.[1] Informed consent increases the ability of subjects to make a decision to participate. It screens out those subjects who believe they might be harmed, it increases trust and respect for science by showing the subjects that they are valued, and reduces the legal liability of the researcher.

Informed consent means a subject must have information to make a decision. How much information does an individual need for informed consent? Diener and Crandall define the amount of information as that amount which a "reasonable or prudent person" would want to know.[1] When should informed consent be obtained? Obviously, prior to the involvement of the subject in the research or any experimental situation. This means, prior to the beginning of any face to face interview, before the experiment begins, or including a consent form with a mailed questionnaire so that the subject can make a decision before taking part in the research.

There are some special populations of individuals who must be given special consideration when informed consent is sought. These are groups of persons who because of their status may not be able to give voluntary or knowledgeable consent. These include children, inmates, or mentally ill individuals.

Deception

Closely related to the issue of informed consent is the use of deception in research which may take many forms. Subjects may give their permission to be studied but may be purposely misinformed about the nature of the research. For example, a researcher might be interested in studying whether male or female police officers differ in their responses to situations of domestic violence. To insure that their behavior is not biased, the researcher may obtain their consent to participate in the study but tell them that the objective of the research is to determine how police react to all incidents which require police intervention. The officers consented to be subjects in the study but were not informed of the true objective of the study.

Subjects may also be deceived about some part of the research process or elements of the research setting. In Milgram's study, subjects were told that a machine they used actually delivered shocks to real people.[9] This was deception. Many experiments make use of deceptive equipment and use confederates, that is individuals who are playing a deceptive role in the research setting.

Subjects may also be completely deceived. That is, they may not know that they are being studied or involved in research at all. Most studies which use this form of deception are field studies. That is, studies of individuals or groups in their natural setting (i.e., The Complete Observer—see Chapter 9). When complete deception is utilized, the researcher takes on a false identity solely for the purpose of studying the group or individual.

The use of deception as a neccessary component of research has been justified in a number of ways. Generally, deception has been deemed necessary to obtain realistic, accurate responses from subjects and as the only means to obtain information on some subjects and/or some forms of behavior. Deception allows the researcher to have methodological control: it allows the researcher to manipulate the environment and influence the behavior of subjects in a way that will evoke realistic responses and enhances external validity—the generalizability of the experimental behavior to the real world or natural setting. Deception is also utilized for pragmatic reasons. Researchers may not have the time, money, or ability to study the behavior except through the use of deception. For example, field studies of juvenile gang behavior or the homeless may not be possible unless the researcher uses deception. Members of these deviant groups do not trust outsiders and are not likely to respond in a natural way around an outsider. Consequently, the researcher may need to masquerade as a member of the group to gather information. Even if a researcher wanted to avoid using deception in these two instances, time and the financial costs might be prohibitive. It would take a long time for the researcher to gain entree into and acceptance by these groups. The cost of this lengthy project could then prevent the research.

Deception may also be practiced for ethical reasons. Miligram in his study of obedience to authority deceived subjects into believing that they were actually shocking and hurting another individual in an adjoining room.[9] This was done because it would not have been appropriate for real shocks to have been delivered and pain inflicted on an actual person. Deception may also be defensible on the evidence of a number of studies related to subject response to deception. A number of researchers have found that subjects do not have strong negative feelings about deception.[3,18] Therefore, they do not feel insulted or harmed when they are told they have been deceived. They accept the deception as a justified part of methodology in a research project.

However, Diener and Crandall cite several studies which suggest that the rates of suspicion among subjects involved in research projects are increasing.[1] The behavior of suspicious subjects may be artificial and bias the results of the research. Even if they are not suspicious about the current study, these subjects may be more likely to try and "play games" with the researcher or "sabotage" the research by responding in a fashion they know is not consistent with their true behavior or normal response. Therefore, the research results may not be sound.

The ethical concerns about deception are that it communicates or validates the acceptability of lying. This may be harmful to researchers and the research enterprise. The use of deception characterizes research as a procedure which uses people as a means to an end or as objects of little value. The respect for research and researchers as well as the willingness of people to be involved in research may be diminished. Deception also runs counter to the inherent principles of informed consent. If deception is utilized, informed consent is either completely or partially circumvented.

Privacy

An ethical problem which is related to all of the three previously identified problem areas is privacy. In our society, we value the rights of individuals and groups of individuals to be free from intrusion into matters that they want to hold confidential. How far this right to privacy extends depends on: the nature of the information or behavior, the setting of the behavior, who is violating the privacy and what is to be done with the information once it has been obtained.

In research projects, these issues of privacy and a violation of this privacy apply. In criminological or criminal justice research the issue of the sensitivity of information is paramount. Much of the data collected by researchers in the area of criminology and criminal justice is sensitive information. Self-report surveys of criminal activity, victimization surveys, studies of police corruption, or studies of criminal career patterns all address information about individuals that could result in harm or embarrassment to the person if their identity were disclosed or discovered. Many studies in criminology and criminal justice also intrude on private settings or privileged relationships. Studies of domestic violence, plea bargaining, gang behavior, or inmate life require the researcher to literally or figuratively intrude on private settings and relationships. Lastly, criminological and criminal justice research is directed toward behaviors or beliefs, values and attitudes that an individual or group may not want disclosed in such a way that the source is identifiable. Correctional managers may not want details about suicides linked to their specific prison. Undetected offenders may not want criminal acts disclosed so that they are identified as the person who committed the crime. Ex-offenders may not want their criminal careers exposed for public scrutiny. It then becomes the responsibility of the researcher to protect the rights of individuals, groups and organizations. This is for the protection of the individual group or organization as well as the researcher and the scientific enterprise.

THE NATURE OF ETHICAL DILEMMAS

These ethical problems present researchers with a number of dilemmas. The researcher must resolve the inherent conflict of these dilemmas as they develop over the course of a research project. Research ethics are a means of achieving and upholding moral values while engaging in research, avoiding research strategies that may endanger these values, and balancing conflicting values that confront the researcher.[1]

The central element of the conflict posed by the research process is how to balance moral values and principles with the need for scientific knowledge and "methodological rigor."[8] The fact that a researcher is responsible for the adherence to ethical standards and accountable for their violation is not denied.[20] The dilemma is posed by issues related to the extent of responsibility, the degree of accountability and to whom the researcher is accountable. Additionally, the point at which the needs of the research process intrude upon or violate the rights and needs of individuals, groups, organizations, and society is a central area of concern.

The research conducted by Marvin E. Wolfgang on delinquency in birth cohorts presents some interesting research issues that pose dilemmas for the social scientist. Wolfgang's[9] initial birth cohort research was a study of approximately ten thousand boys born in 1945 who lived in Philadelphia. The initial study did not result in ethical problems. In 1971, a follow-up study of a ten percent random sample of the cohort was conducted.[10]

The research in the cohorts involved interviews to collect demographic data and self-reported criminal activities. The interviews were conducted prior to the intense concern about research using human subjects. While those interviewed gave their verbal consent, no written informed consent was utilized. The written informed consent was not obtained because (1) the informed consent could not promise legal protection to the subjects should the police or courts want to access to the data and (2) this information might influence the responses of the subject. Nonetheless, the interviewers verbally promised confidentiality, use of the data for exclusively research purposes, and that no individual would be identified in the report.

This research raises a number of ethical concerns.

1. Did the methodological needs of the research outweigh the protection of the subjects?
2. Did publication of the research create greater "risks" for the subjects since publication brings greater visibility?
3. Were the researchers accessories after the fact to the reported criminal?

In this instance, the researcher believed that the likelihood of requests for data was minimal enough to justify publication and to minimize the risk to the subjects. The research was a neutral enterprise not designed to help or hurt subjects and so the researcher was not helping or hindering criminal justice operations.[10] After reading the following sections, how would you answer these questions?

Creating Minimal Risks and Informed Consent

It is generally accepted that researchers have an obligation to conduct their research in such a way that minimal risks will be posed to the subjects. Some decision must be made about the benefits that will follow from the exposure of subjects to situations that could produce harm or put them at risk of harm. Levine has identified five criteria which can be applied by researchers in assessing the degree of risk to subjects posed by the research project.[6]

1. Likelihood: What is the probability that harm will occur?
2. Scrutiny: If harm to the subject occurs, how serious or detrimental will it be?
3. Duration after research: If subjects are harmed, will the injury last past the end of their involvement in the project or will the harm continue and if so, for how long?
4. Reversibility: If harm occurs can the consequences of this harm be reversed or altered?
5. Measures for early detection: Is it possible to build-in procedures to monitor subjects and to identify the inception of harm or the immediate predecessors to harm?

To this list of criteria, Diener and Crandall have added a criterion which would compare the risks of participation in research to the risks of life in general.[1] If the involvement of the subject poses risks comparable to those of everyday life then the risk is justified. If not, the research must be more carefully scrutinized and mechanisms to protect subjects or minimize risks should be invoked. Some of the strategies suggested by these authors are: screening subjects to exclude those with a greater likelihood of harm; attempting to predict harm through pilot studies or role-playing; "assessing and ameliorating harm" by debriefing the subjects after their involvement; providing services to address the harm if it is present or referring subjects these services; and review of the research methodology by colleagues or formal review boards who can scrutinize the research for potential risks to subjects.

These general guidelines are useful tools. However, they may not always resolve the dilemma. All potential harm and its degree of severity and duration cannot be predicted. For example, an inmate agrees to be interviewed for a study of the impact of involvement in prison programs on institutional adjustment. Following the interview the inmate returns to his housing unit and is confronted by a group of irate fellow inmates. The inmates who confront him are convinced that he has been disclosing information about a drug ring that exists in his housing unit. He cannot convince them otherwise. They band together, seriously beat him and he must be hospitalized. Could this type of harm have been anticipated, eliminated, or reduced? Is the researcher responsible? Obviously, if one uses the "everyday life criteria" for life outside the prison, the risks entailed in being interviewed on this topic would be minimal and justified. Should the researcher have used "everyday life within an institution" as a standard? If so, would the researcher have anticipated the potential harm? Similarly, it may not always be possible to adequately screen for an individual's potential to be harmed by involvement in a research project. Nor to determine how long the harm will last.

While it may not always be possible for the researcher to precisely identify the specific risks involved in a research project, the criterion identified by Levine,[6] Diener and Crandall's[1] criteria of the "similarity to life's risks," and the additional safeguard of informed consent, may minimize risks to participants.

As discussed in an earlier section, informed consent is the voluntary participation of subjects in a research project. In making the decision to participate, subjects are informed of the risks involved in the research project prior to their involvement and are given the right to withdraw their consent at any time during the project. This knowledge of risk and adequate information to make an informed decision to participate means that the subjects must have at a minimum, the following information:

1. Purpose of the research.
2. The role of the subjects in the research: What they will be expected to do?
3. Why they were selected as subjects?
4. Information about the procedures: Time, date, place of the research, who will be involved, what will occur (an interview, questionnaire, or observation).
5. Any risks or discomforts suffered during or after the project.
6. Any potential benefits or lack of benefits to the subject.
7. The ability to ask any questions to clarify information about the project or their involvements.
8. The opportunity to discuss their decision with others if they wish.
9. A guarantee that they may withdraw from the project at any time.
10. If the researcher is not able to give them full information prior to their participation, the guarantee that they will be informed in full at the end of their participation.[1]
11. A promise of anonymity so that their identity will be protected.
12. An explanation of how the data from the project will be utilized.
13. The researcher's organizational affiliation and the sponsor of the research, if applicable.

The complexity of informed consent and its importance as a protection for both the subject and the researcher requires that a written document containing this information be utilized. This document is provided to the subject. If the subject agrees to participate, both the subject and the researcher sign the document. The question of when is consent necessary is one which criminal justice and criminological researchers address in a number of different ways. In general, criminal justice researchers who observe public behavior or use public documents are not required to obtain informed consent. However, especially in the case of public documents, they are required to protect the identity of any individuals identified by or named in these documents. If the researcher is interested in potentially sensitive or personal information or information that might be harmful to a subject, informed consent is also required. Similarly, if the research involves exposing the subject to risks, then the informed consent of the subject must be obtained.

What about those instances in which the researcher must use deception to get an accurate subject response? What if the information is only available through the use of deception? In these instances, the methodological and scientific goals of the researcher may be in conflict with the subject's right to privacy and informed consent.

DECEPTION, PRIVACY, AND INFORMED CONSENT

Most deception in criminal justice and criminological research is utilized in field studies. These are studies in which the researcher "enters the world" of his or her subjects and studies their behavior in a natural setting. Klockars raises the question of whether it is possible to conduct field research with deviant subjects or on deviant behavior without employing "morally dubious" means.[5] One of these is deception. Klockars also asks, if researchers employ "morally dubious means" should they be willing to face the consequences and, if so, how should they be made to face the "probability of evil ramifications"—negative consequences for both themselves and their subjects.[5]

People who engage in deviant acts want to avoid detection. Consequently, they perform their acts in a secretive fashion. If a researcher wants to study their behavior, she or he may have to deceive the subjects. This may mean the researcher poses as a member of a deviant group or as someone other than a researcher and the subjects do not even know they are being studied. It may also mean that they are given false information, about the research but know they are participants. For example, Albert Reiss[13,14] wanted to study the treatment of individuals by police officers. Of specific interest were instances of police brutality. Reiss realized that the police officers would not engage in acts of brutality if they knew they were being studied. Reiss deceived the officers. He told them he was studying the citizens' reaction to them rather than visa versa. Could Reiss have gathered data on police brutality if the officers he observed had known the true purpose of his study? Was his deception the only way to collect this data? Was the need for this information great enough to justify the falsehoods involved? These are important questions that each researcher must take into consideration when planning a project of this type.

When studying deviant subjects, problems arise as part of what Klockars has identified as "Dirty Hands Problems."[5] That is, when, as is frequently the case in criminal justice or criminological research, deviant subjects are studied, the researcher must have the trust and confidence of these subjects. If not, they hide their deviant activity. Consequently, the researcher may need to totally or partially deceive these individuals. Whether total, partial, or no deception is involved, the researcher must respect the trust of these subjects. They have a right to privacy and the researcher has an obligation to respect this privacy. The researcher must then be willing not to "blow the whistle"[5] on the deviant acts. The researcher may be required to perform deviant acts to establish trust and/ or to observe the behavior of the deviants. How far does this implied promise of secrecy extend? Do researchers become accessories to criminal acts if they fail to repeat or stop the activities they might observe? What guarantees can they provide their subjects if their records are requested by the courts or other legal or legislative entity? The answers to these questions have important consequences for both researchers and subjects.

RESEARCHERS AND IMMUNITY

Confidentiality between some individuals in certain relationships has been deemed essential and is respected. The attorney-client, doctor-patient, psychologist-client relationships are protected relationships. However, while the researcher-subject relationship also requires confidentiality, it does not have the same legal protections. Researchers are vulnerable to attempts to force them to violate the confidences inherent in the research process. As Nejelski and Lerman have stated, "these demands for confidential research data can cover a range of topics, assume a variety of forms, and come from different types of individuals."[11]

These demands may come in the form of a subpoena from the courts at any stage in civil or criminal proceedings, or from legislative or administrative bodies. Other requests may come from state agents, project sponsors or police agencies as well as other colleagues. While the state, state agency, public official or private individual may have an interest in obtaining access to the information, the researcher has an interest in protecting the confidentiality.

The interests of the researcher in protecting confidentiality are extensive. A "researcher wants free access to all available information about subjects and needs an open atmosphere in which he can collect unbiased data."[11] The subjects want to protect themselves against invasions of privacy. The researcher must provide subjects with a guarantee of anonymity to protect their rights and to gain their consent to participate. Without the promise of confidentiality in the research process, many studies in the area of criminology and criminal justice would not have been conducted. Confidentiality then, not only protects the interests of subjects but also promotes scientific research and the acquisition of knowledge.

A number of strategies have been adopted to protect confidentiality and to make data anonymous. Many researchers use a code number to identify respondents rather than names. Researchers may also destroy data that is identifiable. For example, if interviews with respondents are taped, the researcher may destroy the tapes once they are transcribed. In transcriptions of tapes all names may be eliminated. Similarly, identifiable information will be masked, generalized, or deleted from publications.

The legal rationale for protection of confidentiality is based on the constitutional rights of freedom of expression, privacy, and constitutional rights of the criminal defendant. According to Nejelski and Lerman, "the first amendment ought to be construed to shield confidential data from government demands; indeed, a review of contemporary judicial interpretation suggests that the constitutional freedom of expression presently does protect the researcher-subject relationship." Their review cites: (1) increasing recognition of freedom of expression as a "legal interest" which supersedes the interests of the state in information; (2) the application of freedom of expression as essential to a "free flow of ideas"; and (3) protection of the "information collection stage" by anonymity of subjects if disclosure would "deter publication."[11] These authors also argue that the right to privacy has been expanded by the courts and can be viewed "(1) as tort remedy normally available for the subject's protection; and (2) as a constitutional shield for the confidential researcher-subject relationship."[11]

Generally, if a subject consents to the research and the consent is based on "informed consent," the researcher has a defense against accusations of the violation of privacy. However, as mentioned in an earlier part of this chapter, many times subjects do not know they are being studied. In these instances the researcher may be vulnerable to litigation. Similarly, if the researcher uses identifiable information about the subject in a publication or other public medium the researcher may be liable. In *Melvin v. Reid* (112 Cal. App. 285,297 p. 91 (1931)) a former prostitute won a judgment against a movie producer who filmed and exhibited a movie about her earlier life which used her maiden name.

The right to privacy may also provide protection for the researcher. The fourth amendment protection against search and seizure and the fifth amendment protection against self-incrimination protect the researcher's ability to sustain confidentiality. The protections provided by these two amendments protect the researcher's records and the researcher's right to refuse to testify or respond.

The rights of criminal defendants, expanded in recent years, also protect the researcher. Rights such as that provided by the *Miranda* Ruling (384 U.S. 436,86 S. Ct. 1602, 16 L. Ed. 2d 694) and the applicability of the exclusionary rule protect researchers from coercion and threats in attempts to gain information from them. However, when information about criminal activities are disclosed to a researcher there is a "lack of express legal protection."[11] Researchers are not usually bound by *Miranda* or other criminal defendant protections. To do so would be extremely detrimental to the research process. They are ethically bound to obtain consent in most instances, however in participant observation studies this may be overlooked for the sake of the methodology. Simultaneously, they are vulnerable to a subpoena requiring testimony or records. Consequently, it has been suggested that it is advisable to terminate an interview when a subject discloses information about undetected criminal activity or criminal activity that has not been discontinued.[4] However, this could suppress the quantity and quality of data which a researcher is able to collect, analyze, and disseminate.

Nejelski and Lerman suggest that a remedy which would allow the subject's freedom of expression and privacy to be protected as well as these rights of the researcher is the recognition of a testimonial privilege.[11] This protects the relationship rather than the diverse interests of the researcher and subject as individuals. This would relieve the researcher of a legal requirement to testify about confidential exchanges made in the researcher-subject relationship. These authors argue that this privilege need not be created, only recognized since it is based on the constitutional protections of freedom of expression, privacy and defendant rights. Many such relationships are recognized: attorney-client, psychologist-patient, psychiatrist-patient, newsman-source, and doctor-patient. These relationships represent roles which require a high degree of trust and responsibility for their execution. The same is true of the researcher-subject role. However, to date, no concise rulings from the courts have occurred. Consequently, researchers must be and, if they engage in potentially controversial research, should be aware of the absence of specific legal protections.

PREVENTING AND LIMITING
UNETHICAL RESEARCH

This chapter has discussed the ethical considerations which researchers must take into account when designing and implementing a research project. The legal protections for subjects and consequent legal controls which can be applied to researchers as well as the absence of clear legal protections for researchers have also been identified. What then can be done to prevent unethical research that results in abuses of subjects and the research endeavor? What prevents researchers from violating ethical standards for their own vested interests or the interests of the research tradition?

A number of mechanisms to address and minimize ethically questionable research have been addressed.[1,7,12,19] The usual approaches which have been presented are: (1) professional associations and codes of ethics; (2) governmental guidelines and administrative review process; (3) judicial intervention and legislative statutes; and (4) the development of humanistic morality among researchers.[7]

The development of codes of ethics by professional associations have been discussed by a number of scholars. Diener and Crandall suggest that the development of codes of ethics as have been developed by the American Psychological Association and the American Sociological Association could serve as research guides yet not impose constraints and restrictions which would be too excessive or limiting.[1] Toch believes these codes should be adopted not because they would have a true impact but because they would have a symbolic value.[19] If professional organizations have their own codes and so appear to be "policing" themselves, the probability of having codes imposed by those outside the organization is reduced.

While Toch's position may seem to be a bit cynical, it is nonetheless a pragmatic suggestion. Professional associations may promulgate codes but they have no authority to enforce these codes. Membership in these organizations is voluntary and censure does not necessarily prevent a scientist from conducting research. Therefore, the codes are, at best, only a checklist to be used by the researcher. According to Reynolds they have limited impact.[16] In fact, Douglas has argued they may even act as a screen for researchers to use as a means to avoid scrutiny of their practices.[2]

Government guidelines and administrative review processes are another proposed mechanism of control. The Institutional Review Board which screens research projects was instituted by the Department of Health, Education and Welfare. These boards which also exist at the university level review research projects to assess the procedures involving the use of human subjects. They are an attempt to review research and assess potential harms and protections to eliminate or minimize these harms to human subjects. According to Reynolds they offer an acceptable means of review on a "case-by-case basis."[16] However, other researchers contend that they may be harmful because they reduce the scientist's autonomy and so may inhibit the scientific process.[15] Another potential problem with these boards is that they are only as effective and fair as the members who hold positions on the board. Board members may, like the researchers themselves, be unable to accurately predict harm. They may also be biased toward certain types of research and so be more tolerant of risks in some areas of substantive research.

The use of judicial or statutory means to address and resolve ethical questions also has some support. The primary interest in this area is in the provision of protections to researchers in the form of a "Researcher's Shield Law."[7] A "Shield Law" would provide researchers with some degree of immunity from forced disclosure of research sources. The absence of clear protections in this area as well as the legal grounds for this type of protection have been discussed in the preceding section. While this may be most salient to research in the area of criminology and criminal justice, Reynolds argues that this is not really necessary since few scientists are confronted with this problem.[16] Additionally, Reynolds[16] and Sagarin and Moneymaker[17] argue that no professional relationship has complete immunity. Any attempt to invoke complete immunity may therefore, not be justified. Researchers should not expect to be any more protected than other professionals whose work requires confidentiality.

Finally, some scholars argue that the most effective means of ensuring ethical research is to "increase the research community's sensitivity to humanistic morality."[7] Several authors have presented this option in some form.[1,2,12] The general thesis of these proponents is that the final decision concerning the ethics of a research project rests with the researcher. Consequently, each researcher, in the end, must use his or her own personal values. Specific prescriptions and proscriptions from others may be present but the ultimate decision is based on the researchers morality. In such a highly personalized and individualized process as research, this would seem to inevitably occur. Researchers are human beings who, like all of us, make moral judgments in everyday life. The moral judgments necessary for research are only an extension of personal morality. Researchers should then be trained to identify and scrutinize the research endeavor. They should be skilled in anticipating harm and developing the means to ameliorate or eliminate this harm. They should be acutely aware of the specific, general, long- and short-term consequences of their research. While this is a subjective decision which varies from researcher to researcher there are research practices which can be identified as posing ethical dilemmas and requiring careful review and consideration. These ethical dilemmas include: harm to the subject, the lack of informed consent, confidentiality, misrepresentation of findings, tampering with data, pressure to engage in a specific research project, and restrictions on the dissemination of findings.[7]

While varied orientations on how to promote ethical research exist, it is true that, "laws and codes serve as adjuncts to personal conscience as the major form of ethical control."[1] Laws and codes serve only as guides. Ultimately, each researcher must make a decision based on his or her own conscience.

CONCLUSION

The research process is not conducted in a void. The impact of the project on society, the subjects, and the researcher must be taken into account. Since no detailed, specific legal guidelines exist to address **all** research issues, the ethics of the researcher must direct this review. Many times it may be impossible to foresee all possible outcomes. Nonetheless, it is incumbent upon the researcher to address, as completely as possible, the risks and benefits to society and his or her subject when designing and implementing a research project.

KEY TERMS

Ethics
Potential Harm
Informed Consent
Deception
Privacy
Minimal Risks

"Dirty Hands Problems"
Confidentiality
Protected Relationship
Testimonial Privilege
Professional Code of Ethics
Humanistic Morality
"Researcher's Shield Law"

STUDY GUIDE

1. What are ethics? Why are ethics a research concern?
2. What four general types of ethical problems confront researchers?
3. What type of harm can result from research? How do researchers justify harm? Do you agree?
4. What is informed consent? Why is it important to the research process?
5. How much information is necessary for informed consent?
6. Why is deception used in research? What forms does it take?
7. How does research violate privacy? How do researchers justify this violation?
8. What is the central element of the conflict inherent in research?
9. What criteria can be used to create minimal risks?
10. How does informed consent minimize risks?
11. What ethical problems are posed by the use of deception? How do researchers justify the use of deception? Do you agree?
12. Do researchers have a legally protected relationship with their subjects?
13. Why does a researcher need to be able to protect confidentiality? What strategies are adopted to protect confidentiality?
14. What is the legal rationale for the protection of confidentiality in the research process?
15. What rights to privacy do subjects have? What rights to privacy do researchers have?
16. How would the recognition of a "testimonial privilege" benefit researchers and subjects? How could it be justified?
17. What strategies have been suggested to prevent or limit unethical research?
18. What are the strengths and weaknesses of these strategies? Which do you think is best? Why?

REFERENCES

1. Diener, Edward and Rick Crandall, *Ethics in Social and Behavioral Research,* (Chicago: University of Chicago Press, 1978).
2. Douglas, Jack D., "Living morality versus bureaucratic fiat," pp. 13-34 in Carl Klockars and Finbarr O'Connor (eds.) *Deviance and Decency,* (Beverly Hills, CA: Sage, 1979).
3. Epstein, Yakow M., Svedfeld, Peter, and Stanley J. Silverstein, "Subject's expectations of and reactions to some behaviors of experimenters," *American Psychologist* 28 (1973): 212-221.
4. Kirkpatrick, A.M., "Privileged communication in the correction services," *Criminal Law Quarterly* 7 (1964): 305.
5. Klockars, Carl B. and Finbarr O'Connor, *Deviance and Decency: The Ethics of Research with Human Subjects* (Beverly Hills, CA: Sage, 1979).
6. Levine, Robert, "The role of assessment of risk-benefit criteria in the determination of the appropriateness of research involving human subjects" Paper prepared for the National Commission for the Protection of Human Subjects of Biomedical and Behavioral Research (Bethesda, MD: U.S. Department of Health, Education, and Welfare, 1975).
7. Longmire, Dennis, "Ethical dilemmas in the research setting: A survey of experiences and responses in the criminological community," *Criminology* 21 (1983): 333-348.
8. Menges, Robert J., "Openness and honesty versus coercion and deception in psychological research" *American Psychologist* 28 (1978): 1030-1034.
9. Wolfgang, Marvin E., Robert M. Figlio, and Thorsten Sellin, *Delinquency in a Birth Cohort* (Chicago: University of Chicago Press, 1972).
10. Wolfgang, Marvin E., "Delinquency in two birth cohorts" *American Behavioral Scientist* 27 (1983): 75-86.
11. Wolfgang, Marvin E., "Confidentiality in criminological research and other ethical issues" *Journal of Criminal Law and Criminology* 72 (1981): 75-86.
12. Milgram, Stanley, "Behavioral study of obedience" *Journal of Abnormal and Social Psychology* 67 (1963): 371-378.
13. *Protecting Individual Privacy in Evaluation Research* (Washington, D.C.: National Academy of Sciences, 1975).
14. Nejelski, Paul and Lindsey M. Lerman, "A researcher-subject testimonial privilege: What to do before the subpoena arrives" *Wisconsin Law Review* 4 (1971): 1085-1148.
15. Reiman, Jeffrey, "Research subjects, political subjects, and human subjects" pp. 35-60 in Carl B. Klockars and Finbarr O'Connor (eds.) *Deviance and Decency* (Beverly Hills, CA: Sage, 1979).
16. Reiss, Albert, "Police brutality — answers to key questions" *Transaction* 5 (1968): 10-19.
17. Reiss, Albert, *The Police and the Public,* (New Haven: Yale University Press, 1971).
18. Reiss, Albert, "Governmental regulation of scientific inquiry: Some paradoxical consequences" pp. 61-98 in Carl B. Klockars and Finbarr O'Connor (eds.) *De-*

viance and Decency (Beverly Hills, CA: Sage, 1979).

19. Reynolds, Paul, *Ethical Dilemmas and Social Science Research* (San Francisco, CA: Jossey-Bass, 1979).

20. Sagarin, Edward and James Moneymaker, "The dilemma of researcher immunity" pp. 175-196 in Carl B. Klockars and Finbarr O'Connor (eds.) *Deviance and Decency* (Beverly Hills, CA: Sage, 1979).

21. Sullivan, David S. and Thomas E. Deiker, "Subject-experimenter perceptions of ethical issues in human research" *American Psychologist* 28 (1973): 587-591.

22. Toch, Hans, "Cast the first stone? Ethics as a weapon" *Criminology* 19 (1981): 185-194.

23. Wilkins, Leslie T., "Human subjects—whose subject?" pp. 99-124 in Carl B. Klockars and Finbarr O'Connor (eds.) *Deviance and Decency* (Beverly Hills, CA: Sage, 1979).

24. Zimbardo, Philip, "On the ethics of intervention in human psychological research: With special reference to the Stanford prison study" *Cognition* 2 (1973): 243-256.

CHAPTER FOUR

MEASURING CRIME:
THE VALIDITY AND RELIABILITY
OF CRIME DATA SOURCES

the government are [sic] very keen on amassing statistics. They collect them, raise them to the nth power, take the cube root and prepare wonderful diagrams. But you must never forget that every one of these figures comes in the first instance from the village watchman, who puts down what he damn well pleases.
— Sir Josiah Stamp[36]

Every statistic (and this includes survey as well as police figures) is shaped by the process which operationally defines it, the procedures which capture it, and the organization which processes and interprets it.
— Wesley G. Skogan[52]

T HESE QUOTATIONS accurately reflect the real tensions which criminal justice researchers face. Their basic subject matter, crime and criminality, often defies accurate measurement. In this chapter, we will examine the problems faced in the measurement of crime through the examination of some sources of crime data. First, we must define the key concepts of measurement, validity and reliability.

KEY MEASUREMENT CONCEPTS

The measurement of a societal phenomenon like crime involves the conscious, controlled and rigorous classification of the observations made. Measurement generally involves the assignment of a numerical value to the observation for the simple purpose of counting and the more complex business of statistical analysis of the phenomenon in order to search for causative factors.

The ability and value of a selected form of measurement is directly related to two key concepts. The first, validity, is defined by Nettler[36] as the accuracy with which a measure gauges the concept under consideration. Skogan[52] states that one of the pitfalls concerning validity is that if the designated measurement procedure fails to measure the actual object of interest (i.e., crime), the resulting figure will be inaccurate and meaningless. In other words, does the procedure for measuring crime accurately reflect the amount of crime committed or does it reflect the impact of other factors? For example, does a decline in the number of reported burglaries indicate that a Citizen's Crime Watch Program has succeeded or have citizens suddenly stopped reporting burglaries to the police because they feel that nothing will be done? We will consider these "other factors" in some detail as the different methods of measuring crime are considered.

There are several different types of validity; two of which directly relate to the measurement of crime.[2] The first is termed face validity and it refers to the "common sense" nature of a measure. For example, do "crimes reported to the police" (UCR) seem, on the face of it, to be an accurate indication of crime in society? The second type of validity, content validity, requires that an instrument measures the phenomenon under study. As we shall see, the Uniform Crime Reports contains a "Crime Index" which purports to serve as an indicator of the level of serious crime in America. One of the weaknesses of the Crime Index is that it counts the theft of a bicycle on the same level as a murder. Due to the absence of some way to distinguish the seriousness of crimes, the content validity of the Crime Index is seriously affected. The other form of validity (convergent-discriminant) will be discussed later.

The second key measurement concept, reliability, refers to the consistency with which a measurement device yields the same numbers upon repeated applications.[35] As Pepinsky[37] indicates, a measure is reliable if different people (or the same people at different times) record the event the same way. Reliability deals with the ability to reproduce findings. For example, we can attempt to gauge the extent to which various police patrol teams classify the same events (types of crime) in the same manner.[52] This procedure would be a test of the reliability of crime measurement.

It is important to note that these concepts are interrelated. Validity requires reliability, but a reliable tool may not be a valid one. A gauge that measures consistently may still not be measuring what it is supposed to count.[36] The accurate measurement of crime for purposes of policy analysis requires careful attention to these concepts — validity and reliability. Naturally, if the selected indicator of crime fails on one or both counts, the subsequent analysis will suffer and be misleading at best.

With these concepts in mind, let us turn to a consideration of some of the standard sources of information about crime and criminality. They follow a generally common-sense point of view about acquiring information about crime. If one wishes to obtain data about crime, one would either go to the police (Uniform Crime Reports), to victims (National Crime Survey) or to the offenders themselves (Self-Report Studies). The assessment of these sources in terms of their validity and reliability requires close attention so that the criminal justice researcher can make the best possible choice in the selection of a crime measure. As we shall see, each measure has potential problems regarding validity and reliability.

THE UNIFORM CRIME REPORTS (UCR)

The Uniform Crime Reporting program, compiled by the Federal Bureau of Investigation, is the oldest source of crime statistics in America. Enacted by Congressional legislation in 1930, the UCR program is a voluntary, national program which is dependent upon the cooperation of law enforcement agencies. Their contribution of reported crimes (crimes known to the police) is published each year. Zolbe[58] reports that after more than five decades of operation, UCR contributors number more than 15,000 and cover in excess of 220 million inhabitants, representing 98 percent of the U.S. population. There is no doubt that the prestige of the FBI facilitates the collection of these data. It is doubtful that any other agency could enjoy such success and obtain such cooperation from law enforcement agencies across the country.

Index Crimes

The UCR program has a number of distinctive characteristics. First, there is a procedure which attempts to standardize crime statistics in order to transcend differences between jurisdictions in terms of their legal definitions. Otherwise, a burglary in one jurisdiction may be classified as a misdemeanor theft in another. To accomplish this goal, the committee on Uniform Crime Records established a standard classification of crime to be used for purposes of reporting offenses known to the police. The selected crimes were those that: (1) were serious in nature, (2) were most likely to come to the attention of the police with sufficient regularity to provide an adequate basis for comparison and (3) were geographically pervasive.[58] These offenses became known as Part I offenses: murder and non-negligent manslaughter, forcible rape, robbery, aggravated assault, burglary, larceny-theft, motor vehicle theft and, beginning in 1978, arson. These offenses were traditionally referred to as "crime index" offenses and they came to be used as a national indicator of crime much like the cost of living index is for the U.S. economy.[57]

Selected UCR Findings

For our purposes, we will focus upon the Crime Index, although the UCR does contain data on other material as well. Again, it must be stressed that the number of index crimes presented reflects the volume of serious crime which was known to the police. That is, the crime was either reported to, or directly discovered by the police. A summary of the data on the crime index for 1983 is presented in Table 4.1.

The data in Table 4.1 reveal that the UCR contains two basic forms of crime information: the actual count of crimes reported to the police and the offense rate per 100,000 inhabitants. Each year, these data are compared to figures from the preceding year and the percent change is noted. The crime rate per 100,000 is the only attempt made by the UCR to control for the effect of an important variable — the size of the population (i.e., Other variables which could affect the number of crimes reported to the police, but which are not controlled for in the UCR include: population density, age, mobility of population, economic and cultural conditions, climate, strength of law enforcement agencies, administrative and investigative emphases of law enforcement, attitudes of the citizenry toward crime, and the crime reporting practices of the citizenry) upon the incidence of reported crime. This step is taken to make it somewhat easier to make limited comparisons of crime rates across jurisdictions, regions and other cities in the country.

The data also reveal a pattern of declining crime rates between the years 1980 and 1981 — a reversal of the trend of the past twenty years. Only robbery increased nationwide. However, before any dramatic conclusions can be drawn, it is necessary to consider the factors which affect

TABLE 4-1

Crime Index Offenses Reported in the United States, 1980-81

Index Offenses	Year	Number of Offenses	Percent Change	Rate per 100,000 Inhabitants	Percent Change
Murder and Non-Negligent Manslaughter	1980	23,044		10.2	
			−2.3		−3.9
	1981	22,516		9.8	
Forcible Rape	1980	82,088		36.4	
			−0.7		−2.2
	1981	81,536		35.6	
Robbery	1980	548,809		243.5	
			+4.6		+2.9
	1981	574,134		250.6	
Aggravated Assault	1980	654,957		290.6	
			−1.7		−3.3
	1981	643,720		280.9	
Burglary	1980	3,759,193		1668.2	
			−0.5		−2.2
	1981	3,739,821		1632.1	
Larceny-Theft	1980	7,112,657		3156.3	
			+0.6		−1.1
	1981	7,154,541		3122.3	
Motor Vehicle Theft	1980	1,114,651		494.6	
			−3.6		−5.2
	1981	1,073,988		468.7	
Arson	1980	N/A			
			N/A	N/A	N/A
	1981	97,202			

Source: Federal Bureau of Investigation: *Uniform Crime Reports for the United States.* Washington, D.C.: U.S. Department of Justice, 1981, p. 6-35.

the validity of the UCR and ultimately the researcher's ability to make proper use of this data set.

Limitations of the Uniform Crime Reports

It is obvious that the number of crimes reported to the police represents only a portion of the actual amount of crime actually committed. The basic problem is that it is difficult, if not impossible, to gauge the amount of unreported crime. This problem, which is common to all the attempts to measure the incidence of crime, is termed the "dark figure of crime."

An examination of the chain of events leading to the reporting and recording of a crime reveals some of the sources of error in UCR statistics. Seidman and Couzens[46] offer the following description:

1. An event occurs, which could be interpreted as a crime.
2. It, or its consequence, is observed, by the victim or perhaps by someone else (i.e., neighbor or the police themselves).
3. The victim (or observer) notifies the police.
4. The police decide whether the reported action is to be considered a crime and, if so, how it should be described.
5. Sometimes, this description is reviewed (and can be dismissed) at another point in the police hierarchy.
6. The police decide which of the FBI categories is appropriate.
7. The statistics are made public.

In short, the sources of invalidity in the UCR statistics can be attributed to three basic sources: factors influencing the reporting of the crime to the police, recording practices of the police themselves, and subsequent problems in the official presentation and interpretation of the UCR statistics.

The first source of invalidity which influences the reporting of crimes to the police is the attitude of the victim. For example, McClintock[35] lists the possible circumstances in which victims are unlikely to report a crime to the police:

1. The victim consents or agrees to the act (i.e., gambling, drug use, prostitution).
2. The victim believes the crime is trivial.
3. The victim does not wish to embarrass the offender who may be a relative, school friend, acquaintance, or fellow employee.
4. The victim is in an embarrassing situation (i.e., the married man on a business trip who is robbed by a prostitute).
5. The victim does not regard the law enforcement process as effective.
6. The victim (or loser) is unaware that he/she is involved in crime due to the skill of the offender.

In this fashion, victims could selectively report crimes to the police and could thus affect subsequent UCR crime rates.

The second source of invalidity is that the police selectively act upon (and hence record) certain events as crime. Part of the police procedure in this area is to "unfound" crimes. Unfounding is defined as the process in which events are excluded:[31]

> from crime records for want of any plausible evidence that a crime was in fact committed . . . [The police] are in a position to provide some independent corroboration of a citizen's complaints and to eliminate those misfortunes that do not amount to crimes (e.g., the abusive landlord) or those fantasies that have no basis in fact (e.g., the imagined prowler).

When the crime is founded, the police have the power to make an arrest. Studies of police arrest practices have demonstrated that the decision to arrest is influenced by:[1] the seriousness of the crime, the expressed preference of the complainant (arrest or release of the suspect), the relationship between the complainant and the suspect (more likely to report strangers), and the attitude of the complainant towards the police. Recognition of these factors has led Quinney[40] to conclude that UCR statistics reflect the policies and behaviors of the police themselves and should be considered as "society's production figures" on crime rather than an accurate indication of how much crime exists at a particular time.

Even when police agencies have received information about a crime, their recording practices have an effect upon the accuracy of the UCR statistics. Some of the problem is due to differences, or mistakes made in the classification of offenses under UCR categories. This problem was indicated in a study by Ferracuti, Hernandez, and Wolfgang.[19] These authors surveyed 86 Puerto Rican personnel directly involved in crime reporting and asked them to identify and classify 22 crime stories and rank them in order of their seriousness. It was discovered that only the four crimes of murder, abandonment of children, prostitution, and violation of liquor laws were correctly identified by all subjects. The largest number of errors were recorded by the crime of robbery (41% wrong). The authors concluded that errors in recording are a relevant factor in any reference to crime statistics and that their evidence is additional proof of the low validity of crime reporting statistics and the need for specific training of police personnel.

Since police agencies have direct control over their crime recording policies and practices, they are also in a position to manipulate these figures in such a way that their performance will be viewed in a positive light. Seidman and Couzens.[46] studied UCR crime rate figures for Washington, D.C. to determine whether a crime suppression program instituted at the behest of the chief (and the Nixon administration) or a change in crime recording practices by the department had produced a decrease in the amount of reported crime. The authors focused upon three Index Crimes (Larceny-theft, Burglary and Robbery) because they, due to the ambiguity of the UCR definitions, offered the best opportunity for manipulation. For example, with larceny-theft, the key aspect in the classification process is the dollar value of the stolen property—the cut-off point is $50. Thus, through property valuation, the police can partially determine the level of UCR statistics and can "downgrade" offenses in order to suit their purposes. Statistical analysis of the D.C. UCR statistics for this time period in comparison to other cities revealed that "at least part of the decline in the crime statistics is attributable to the increased downgrading of larcenies and, to a lesser extent, burglaries." In short, the UCR reporting system could be manipulated and is open to tampering by police departments who wish to do so for political reasons.

Given these influences upon victims and the police in terms of crime reporting, the validity of UCR data is directly related to the type of crime under consideration. For example, a crime like rape is likely to be underreported because of the social pressures placed upon the victim. On the other hand, victims are likely to report burglaries because of home insurance requirements. Similarly, homicide is unlikely to go unreported by the police or the public because of the severity of the offense. For this reason, researchers must consider the type of crime under analysis when utilizing UCR data.

Finally, the presentation of UCR statistics can often lead to misinterpretation. First, the Crime Index, which is meant to portray the level of serious crime in this country, contains no information concerning white collar offenses, distorting the impact of "street level" crime, and thus giving a false impression of the seriousness of crime in America.[57] The Index also counts attempts on the same level as completed acts with certain crimes (i.e., forcible rape, robbery, aggravated assault, burglary, and motor vehicle theft). The Index also has problems with multiple offenses—when more than one offense occurs, the one which is considered "more serious" (higher in the rank order of the Index offenses) is the only offense counted. Wolfgang[57] cites the following example and directions given from the 1960 UCR Handbook:

1. **Problem:** A holdup man forces a husband and his wife to get out of their automobile. He shoots the husband, gun whips and rapes the wife and leaves the automobile after taking the money from

the husband. The husband dies as a result of the shooting.

2. **Solution:** In the problem, we can recognize robbery, aggravated assault, rape, murder, as well as auto theft and larceny . . . From the several crimes in the problem, you recognize . . ., murder and non-negligent manslaughter as the first crime on the list. Stop at that classification — it is the only one that will be used for scoring the problem.

The Index also has problems counting the number of victims of a crime. Here, again a particular counting method is used: for personal crimes (murder, forcible rape, aggravated assault, robbery), the number of listed offenses equals the number of persons injured and for property crimes (burglary, larceny-theft, and motor vehicle theft) each operation is a single offense — the number of victims is not indicated.[43] As previously mentioned, the Crime Index totals are misleading because each offense represents one unit regardless of the seriousness of the offense — a homicide has the same value as the theft of a $51 bicycle. Thus, the total Crime Index fails to represent a clear picture of crime severity.

The figures and graphs which summarize the UCR data affect the manner in which it is interpreted. Two figures which were presented earlier, the percentage change this year and the rate per 100,000 are particularly inaccurate since no attempt is made to control for the effects of changes in the size of the U.S. population. Prior to the 1981 findings, the UCR was particularly susceptible to the charge that "the message the Report most obviously wishes to broadcast is that crime has greatly increased."[57] Here, the most blatant offender is Figure 4-1, the Crime Clock. Regardless of the caveat in small print at the bottom of the chart, the purpose of this graph is to alarm the reader as to the extent of American crime. Such presentations can only serve to color the reader's interpretation of the other statistics contained in the report.

Conclusions Concerning UCR

Given these weaknesses, what is the value of the UCR to criminal justice researchers? As a data source, the UCR consists of crimes known to the police (KTP) and highlights the Index Offenses. Crime rates per 100,000 inhabitants are also reported.

The limitations of UCR data include the fact that the reporting practices of victims and the police are subject to some pressures. Police recording practices also affect the quality of the data and since police agencies are responsible for data collection, the data can be manipulated.

FIGURE 4-1

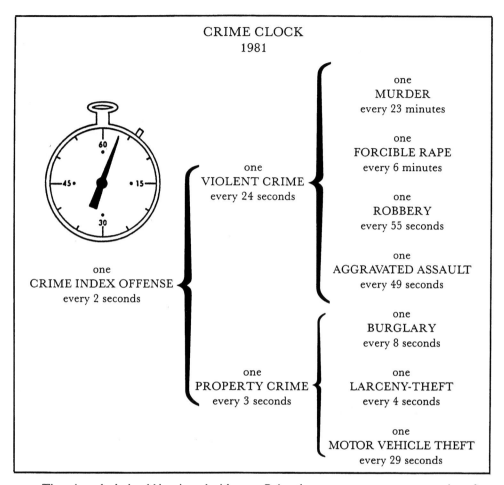

CRIME CLOCK
1981

one
CRIME INDEX OFFENSE
every 2 seconds

one
VIOLENT CRIME
every 24 seconds

one
MURDER
every 23 minutes

one
FORCIBLE RAPE
every 6 minutes

one
ROBBERY
every 55 seconds

one
AGGRAVATED ASSAULT
every 49 seconds

one
PROPERTY CRIME
every 3 seconds

one
BURGLARY
every 8 seconds

one
LARCENY-THEFT
every 4 seconds

one
MOTOR VEHICLE THEFT
every 29 seconds

The crime clock should be viewed with care. Being the most aggregate representation of UCR data, it is designed to convey the annual reported crime experience by showing the relative frequency of occurrence of the Index Offenses. This mode of display should not be taken to imply a regularity in the commission of the Part I Offenses; rather, it represents the annual ratio of crime to fixed time intervals.

Source: Federal Bureau of Investigation: *Uniform Crime Reports for the United States.* Washington, D.C.: U.S. Department of Justice, 1981, p. 5.

Finally, the data is presented in the UCR (i.e., the Crime Clock) in a misleading fashion.

It is important to recognize that the UCR statistics are the product of the interaction between offenders, victims, and the police. Zolbe[57] reminds us that many of the constraints and limitations of the UCR data exist because the UCR was designed and created to meet the needs of the police, not the academic community.

An awareness of the limitations of the UCR data should enable researchers to gauge them accurately and utilize them properly. The UCR does provide a nationwide data set on a yearly basis for different cities and states. On this scope, there is no substitute for this source of crime information.

THE NATIONAL CRIME SURVEY (NCS)

A second possible source of information on the extent of crime is the victim. In fact, interviewing victims offers a greater potential for accuracy than police crime reports since the researcher is eliminating the "middleman" (the police) and going directly to the primary source of information (the victim). Such an approach can help to overcome problems of non-reporting and thus illuminate the "dark figure of crime."

Since 1972, the National Crime Survey has been conducted for the Bureau of Justice Statistics (formerly the Law Enforcement Assistance Administration) by the U.S. Bureau of the Census. Fienberg[20] has identified eight primary purposes of the NCS:

1. To measure the incidence of crime.
2. To measure the changes in crime rates over time.
3. To characterize the socioeconomic aspects of criminal events and their victims.
4. To identify high-risk subgroups in the population and to estimate the rate of multiple victimization.
5. To provide a measure of victim risk.
6. To calibrate the UCR data produced by the FBI.
7. To index changes in the reporting behavior of victims.
8. To measure the effectiveness of new criminal justice programs (The city surveys were initiated for exactly this reason).

The methodology utilized in this survey is particularly relevant to the student since it demonstrates a number of significant principles including: sampling, interviewing techniques and the structured questionnaire. These topics will be referred to in other chapters of this text.

Features of the NCS

The NCS is based upon a scientifically-selected, probability sample (stratified, multi-stage, cluster design) of housing units. The panel consists of addresses of six independently selected samples of about 10,000 households with 22,000 individuals (total 60,000 households and 130,000 individuals). Interviewers return to the same housing units every six months for information. If the occupants have moved, the new residents are interviewed. Housing units in the panel are visited a maximum of seven times, after which they are rotated out of the panel and replaced by a new, independent probability sample.[21] In sum, the National Crime Survey is designed to elicit responses on criminal victimization which are representative of the nation as a whole.

The household portion of the survey focuses upon some of the same offenses covered by the UCR crime index (burglary, motor vehicle theft, rape, robbery, assault and larceny of property and larceny from the person). In each household, a knowledgeable adult is selected to answer background questions about the household. Each individual household member over age 14 is personally interviewed about victimizations he or she may have suffered during the past year.

The validity of the information provided by the respondents is limited by two particular types of memory bias. First, there is the problem of forgetting (memory decay)—the failure to recall an event at all. Victims tend to forget crime incidents as a function of the time period between when the crime occurred and when the interview takes place. Thus, the longer the time lag, the greater the potential of forgetting.[45] The second problem is called telescoping. As Gottfredson and Hindelang[24] have written, telescoping can be forward or backward: an event may be remembered as having occurred more recently than it actually did, or it may be remembered as having occurred in the past. Telescoping would affect the results of the survey by including events which should not be included or by excluding those which should be included.

In order to deal with these problems, the NCS uses a "bounding technique" in which respondents are interviewed every six months. In this fashion, the first interview serves as a benchmark and the records of each successive interview aids in the avoidance of duplication in the reports and as a check against which responses can be ascertained.

In addition to the previously mentioned crimes, the NCS also provides data about the characteristics of the victim, the crime itself, and, with certain crimes, about offenders. Demographic characteristics of the victim are presented, including: age, race, sex, educational level, and income. Information on the characteristics of the crime are: where and when it occurred, the extent of injury and economic loss suffered by the victim, the relationship between the victim and the person committing the crime, the characteristics of the offender as perceived by the victim and whether or not the crime was reported to the police. Unlike the UCR, NCS does not provide data on particular cities and counties, but it does provide data on suburban and urban victims and crimes, and for four major geographic regions. It also presents NCS victimization rates per 1,000 population.[11]

A recent feature of the NCS which is designed to serve an attention-getting purpose similar to the UCR crime index is the measure "households touched by crime." It is officially defined as a "new statistical indicator measuring the pervasiveness of crime." It takes into account all of the six previously-mentioned crimes.[12]

Selected NCS Findings

In its annual report, the NCS provides a summary of its findings along with all of the raw data in tabular form. In 1983, the following patterns were reported:[13]

- Violent crime rates were much higher for males than females. For example, men were robbed or assaulted about twice as often as women.
- For crimes of violence and theft, persons aged 12-24 had the highest victimization rates.
- Blacks experienced the highest rate of violent crime, especially for robbery.
- Black males had the highest rate of violent crime victimization and white females had the lowest.
- Unemployed persons (regardless of race) had a higher rate of violent crime victimization than employed persons.
- Persons living in cities had higher rates of victimization than individuals living in suburban or rural areas.
- Total burglary rates were higher by whites across all income levels.
- Home renters were more likely to be the victim of household property crimes (i.e., burglary, larceny) than were home owners.
- The majority of violent crimes (59%) were committed by strangers. There was some evidence that whites were the victims of violent crimes involving strangers at a slightly higher rate than blacks.
- Most violent crimes were committed within racial groups: white to white (78%) and black to black (87%) yet 55 percent of the violent crimes committed by black offenders were against white victims.
- Half of all violent crimes took place at night while incidents of personal theft were most likely to occur during the day.

- Streets were the most common site for violent crime and personal larceny with contact.
- The majority of violent crimes did not involve the use of a weapon, however, weapons were frequently used in violent confrontations between strangers.
- Robbery victims who tried to use force, tried to get help or attempted to frighten the offender were more likely to be injured.
- One out of ten violent crime victims incurred medical expenses.
- Nearly half the losses from personal crimes were valued at less than $50 per victimization.
- Nearly half of all violent crime victimizations and 37 percent of the household crimes were reported to the police in 1983.
- For violent crimes the most frequent reason given for reporting the crime was to prevent it from happening again. Among property crimes, the most frequent reason given was the desire to recover property. The most frequent reason for non-reporting for all types of crime was that the offense was not important enough to call the police.

Finally in 1984, more than 22 million households (about 27% of the households in the nation) were touched by crime. The Bureau of Justice Statistics[10] has stated that this indicator is "one of pervasiveness and consistency." As Table 4.2 indicates, the proportion of American households which experienced crime has been declining over the last ten years.

Another summary statistic of the NCS is the victimization rate per 1,000 citizens. These rates are also given for different groups of individuals by age, income level, sex, education, and locality of residence. Table 4.3 presents a summary of victimization rates per 1,000 for all crimes covered under the NCS. Note that between 1980 and 1981, virtually all victimization rates (with the exception of household larceny) increased. However, it must be remembered that not all groups have the same rate of victimization and that victimization rates by group may present a clearer picture of the threat of crime.

Advantages of NCS

As we shall see, the NCS is consistently compared to the UCR in terms of its data and its utility. Several authors have identified the advantages of utilizing the NCS data:[21,51]

1. It can be used to assess the costs of crime attributable to direct

TABLE 4.2

HOUSEHOLDS TOUCHED BY CRIME, 1975-1984:

Number and percent distribution by type of crime

	1975	1976	1977	1978	1979	1980	1981	1982	1983	1984
Percent of households touched by:										
All crimes	32.0	31.5	31.3	31.3	31.3	30.0	24.9	29.2	27.4	26.0
Rape	0.2	0.2	0.2	0.2	0.2	0.2	0.2	0.2	0.1	0.2
Robbery	1.4	1.2	1.2	1.1	1.2	1.2	1.1	1.4	1.1	1.0
Assault	4.5	4.4	4.7	4.6	4.8	4.4	3.9	4.5	4.2	4.1
Personal Larceny	16.4	16.2	16.3	16.2	15.4	14.2	11.5	13.8	13.0	12.3
Burglary	7.7	7.4	7.2	7.2	7.1	7.0	6.1	6.9	6.1	5.5
Household Larceny	10.2	10.3	10.2	9.9	10.8	10.4	8.5	9.6	8.9	8.5
Motor Vehicle Theft	1.8	1.6	1.5	1.7	1.6	1.6	1.3	1.6	1.4	1.4
Households touched by crime (thousands)	23,377	23,504	23,741	24,277	24,730	24,222	—	24,989	23,621	22,786
Households in U.S. (thousands)	73,123	74,528	75,904	77,578	78,964	80,622	—	85,178	86,146	87,693

Source: Bureau of Justice Statistics Bulletin: *The Prevalence of Crime.* Washington, D.C.: U.S. Department of Justice, March, 1981, p. 1. Bureau of Justice Statistics Bulletin: *Households Touched by Crime, 1982-84.* Washington, D.C.: U.S. Department of Justice, 1983-85.

TABLE 4.3

VICTIMIZATION RATES PER 1000 FOR
PERSONAL AND HOUSEHOLD CRIMES, 1980-1983

Personal Sector	1980	1981	1982	1983	Percent Change
Crimes of Violence	33.3	35.3	34.3	31.0	+ 6.9
Rape	0.9	1.0	0.8	0.8	+11.1
Robbery	6.6	7.4	7.1	6.0	− 9.1
Assault	25.8	27.0	26.4	24.1	− 6.6
Aggravated	9.3	9.6	9.3	8.0	−14.4
Simple	16.5	17.3	17.1	16.2	− 1.8
Crimes of Theft	83.0	85.1	82.5	76.9	− 7.3
Larceny with Contact	3.0	3.3	3.1	3.0	0
Larceny without Contact	80.0	81.9	79.5	74.0	− 7.5
Household Sector					
Household Burglary	84.3	87.9	78.2	70.0	−17.0
Household Larceny	126.5	121.0	113.9	105.2	−16.8
Motor Vehicle Theft	16.7	17.1	16.2	14.6	−12.6

Source: Bureau of Justice Statistics Bulletin: *Criminal Victimization 1983.* Washington, D.C.:
U.S. Department of Justice, June, 1984, p. 3.
Bureau of Justice Statistics: *Criminal Victimization in the United States, 1982 and 1983.*
Washington, D.C.: U.S. Department of Justice, 1984 and 1985.

losses, injuries, insurance premiums and crime reduction measures.

2. The survey permits collection of crime data, independent of police agencies and makes it possible to measure crimes reported
   and unreported to the police.

3. It makes it possible to discover who calls the police and why, what
   happens when they do (and do not) and whether they are satisfied
   with the results.

4. It provides more detailed data about crime incidents and victims
   which can be of particular use in terms of eliciting descriptions of
   the *modus operandi* of offenders including the use of weapons,
   means of access to targets, the efficiency of alarms, and the utility
   of resistance.

It is clear that these advantages are directly attributable to the nature of
the data and its source, the victims themselves.

Limitations of NCS

This does not mean that the NCS represents the most valid and reliable source of crime data. There are several limitations, in addition to telescoping and forgetting, surrounding their use. The most thorough critique of the NCS approach is provided by James Levine[34] and it deserves our full attention.

To Levine, the victimization survey has become a sort of "talisman" — a foolproof and unquestioned way of determining the actual amount of crime that is committed. Listing the possible sources of NCS invalidity, Levine begins with the potential for false reporting by respondents (other than telescoping and forgetting):

1. Lying: If people are not trustworthy in talking about their voting behavior, financial position, business practices, sex lives, and the academic progress of their children, why take for granted their reporting about crime?
   Motives: To gain the sympathy of the interviewer respondents may feel obligated to give the interviewer what they think he is seeking.
2. The questions asked may elicit different recollections from different people.
3. People are unaware of legal definitions and may interpret "trivial grievances" as crime.
4. Respondents may be unwilling to discuss victimizations of an embarrassing nature or crimes which are committed by persons known to the victim.

Second, Levine identifies the following sources of interviewer bias:

1. Although each interviewer follows the same questionnaire, interviewers may still unwittingly cue respondents to answer in a particular way.
2. The interviewer could record answers incorrectly or make up answers to questions which the respondents do not wish to answer.
3. Interviewer self-interest: Keeping their jobs, avoiding work which is unpleasant, pleasing superiors by producing results in keeping with what they think is most advantageous to the organization (i.e., uncovering unreported crime), and self-serving purposes (i.e., altering responses to relieve the tedium of a steady stream of negative answers).

Finally, Levine notes that there is a possibility that the same types of errors may be made in the coding of the data. He also recommends that response error be checked by using a sample of alleged victimizations and then determining if a crime actually occurred.

Conclusions Concerning the NCS

Obviously, the NCS is not a foolproof source of crime information. As Garofolo and Hindelang[21] have noted:

> . . . the NCS is not an ultimate data source. It has many limitations that can only be overcome and gaps that can only be filled by treating it as a complement to, rather than as a replacement for, other data sources.

The obvious strength of the NCS is that it attempts to go directly to the victims of crime and overcome the problems of under or non-reporting. It includes data concerning victims; their personal characteristics, where and when the crime took place, and the nature and extent of the victimization. It also includes information on "households touched by crime" during the past year. The NCS thus provides information on criminal victimization on a nationwide basis.

The scope of the NCS, however, is one of its basic weaknesses. The data presented is representative of the nation as a whole and is not broken down by state, city, or region of the country. Other limitations of the NCS include its financial cost, the problems associated with victim recall (telescoping, forgetting, lying) and the potential for interviewer bias.

The deciding factor in the selection of NCS over UCR data (or vice versa) should be the needs of the particular study. The determination of their strengths, weaknesses, and differences in terms of the treatment of the data should help the researcher make a choice. A comparison summary of the UCR and the NCS is presented in Table 4.4.

SELF-REPORT STUDIES

The final possible source of crime information is to go directly to the offender. Like the victimization survey, this technique is designed to uncover unreported crime. It also questions the validity of official crime statistics by examining the criminal justice process. System-produced data may have "holes" in it: some persons are arrested and sanctioned while others who commit the same crime are not. Nettler[36] lists the various methods in which self-report studies can be conducted:

1. By asking people to complete anonymous questionnaires.
2. By asking people to complete anonymous questionnaires identified in a circuitous fashion and validated against later interviews or police records.

3. By asking people to confess criminal acts on signed questionnaires validated against police records.
4. By having people complete anonymous questionnaires identified by number and validated against follow-up interviews and the threat of polygraph.
5. By interviewing respondents.
6. By interviewing respondents and validating their responses against official records.

We shall examine two such studies which utilized different techniques and subjects.

Gold: "Undetected Delinquent Behavior"

The purpose of Gold's study[22] was to determine whether the label of juvenile delinquent was placed upon youths along social class lines. Specifically, the research questions were: how many delinquent acts do juveniles commit, are there any actual differences along class lines or are lower class youths simply sanctioned at a higher rate than other youths?

Gold pursued the questions through the use of a random sample of 600 teenagers (age 13-16, 522 respondents) living in the Flint, Michigan school district. College students were trained to interview youngsters of the same sex and race as themselves and were instructed to refuse the assignment if they were acquainted with the respondents. The respondents and their parents received a letter from Gold stating that they had been selected for a study of "what teenagers do in their spare time." Interviewers arranged to drive each respondent to a community center or facility near their home in order to conduct the interview under standardized conditions. During the course of this drive, the actual purpose of the study was revealed to the teenager and though given the opportunity to withdraw (6% did), respondents were assured that they had been selected at random for the study and that their replies would be kept anonymous and confidential.

During the course of the interview, the subjects were asked, through the use of cards and a sortboard, to identify which of some 51 acts (ranging from truancy, trespass, creating damage, hitting your father, lying, stealing, drinking beer, fighting, arson, smoking, taking a car, fornication, and carrying weapons) they had committed (never, more than three years ago, or in the last three years).

In order to ascertain the validity of responses, Gold made use of a "criterion group" of 125 youngsters about whose delinquency Gold had already obtained reliable data from a group of informants. The only facts which were considered reliable were those events which the informants had witnessed themselves or the details of which the respondent had confessed to the informant.

Using the information obtained from the group of informants, Gold constructed the following typology of the 125 criterion group respondents.

1. **The truthteller:** Youngsters who told what the relevant informant had told the researchers or if he told them more recent offenses of the same type or about more serious offenses (90/ 125 = 72%).

2. **The concealer:** Youngsters who did not confess to an offense about which an informant told (22/125 = 17%).

3. **The questionable:** Youths who did not exactly match offenses with the informant (13/125 = 11%).

Gold reported that the offenses most often concealed by the male criterion group were breaking and entering, property destruction and carrying a concealed weapon. Gold also recognized that, even with the use of the criterion group, two potential problems remained—youths who exaggerated their behavior and those who committed their offenses alone.

Selected Findings

Gold suspected that "the rich kids get away with delinquency and the poor kids get records." He made use of the self-report technique in the hope that it would be free of the "selectivity which exists in the records of police, courts, and social agencies." However, the results of the study revealed that social status was inversely related to delinquency—lower status youngsters committed delinquent acts more frequently than higher status youngsters. Yet, when a comparison was made between the interview results and the official records, it was discovered that the official records exaggerated the delinquency of lower class youths. The lower class boys were five times more likely to be booked than the higher status boys.

Petersilia, Greenwood, and Lavin, "Criminal Careers of Habitual Offenders"

The bulk of self-report studies, like Gold's, have focused upon juvenile delinquency as the subject of study.[28] However, this method can also be used with adult populations. Research conducted by Petersilia, Green-wood, and Lavin[38] of the Rand Corporation represents a recent attempt to use the self-report method as a means of uncover crime. Here, the focus of the study was habitual offenders and the key research hypothesis was "How many crimes do habitual offenders actually commit?" The policy implications of this study revolved around the issue of incapacitation, namely "Can crime be prevented by incarcerating habitual offenders for longer periods of time?" The research represents a direct test of the rationale behind habitual offender and mandatory sentencing legislation.

The study focuses upon the criminal careers of 49 inmates from a medium-security California prison. In order to be considered for the study, inmates must have been convicted of armed robbery (indicator of serious criminal conduct) and have served at least one prior prison term (indicator of persistent criminal activity).

Each interviewee was sent a formal notice of the interview and the purpose of the study was explained to them. One inmate was transferred, four did not appear at the interview station and one interview was discarded because the inmate appeared to be "under the influence" at the time of the interview. The researchers utilized a highly-structured questionnaire which collected data on 200 variables. In addition, the questionnaire corresponded to three career periods: (a) Juvenile (first offense, incarceration to age 18), (b) Young Adult (from release after first juvenile incarceration through first adult incarceration), and (c) Adult (from release after first adult incarceration to the current prison term). During the interview, only the inmate and the interviewer were present with no correctional officer within hearing distance.

Petersilia[39] has explicity discussed the method used to attempt to validate the inmate responses. Respondents confirmed each period of incarceration which the researchers recorded from the inmates' official criminal record ("rap sheet") and supplied information on how long each of the incarcerations lasted. Each self-reported arrest or conviction item was validated only if the official record showed an arrest or conviction for the same type of crime during the specific dates identified as the beginning and end of each crime period. In short, the rap sheet was used as a benchmark to gauge the accuracy of the inmates' responses. If they correctly reported the offenses known to the researchers, the assumption was that they would be truthful about the nature and number of offenses for which they were not apprehended. Offenders in the study reported

63 percent of the arrests, 74 percent of the convictions, and 88 percent of the incarcerations contained in their official records.

Other tests of validity were also conducted.[39] For the two adult career periods, the offenders reported roughly half of their official arrests and convictions. The theory that, if the respondent wants to present himself in the best light, he will underreport the most stigmatizing offenses was not supported. In fact, just the opposite pattern was discovered by the researchers. The offenses which were less serious (i.e., grand larceny, auto theft) were less accurately reported. It was also found that the inmates, apparently due to their desire to appear "rehabilitated," underreported those offenses which occurred in the time period closest to the interview. Overall, the respondents reported approximately 50 percent of their adult and 75 percent of their juvenile arrests and convictions.

Selected Findings

As a group, the 49 respondents admitted that they were responsible for over 10,500 crimes. The top three categories were drug sales (3,620), burglary (2,331), and auto theft (1,492). Since the average criminal career was about 20 years long and half of this time was spent in prison, the average respondent committed 20 crimes every year they were on the street. It was also reported that the number of self-reported offenses committed per month of street crime noticeably declined as the group grew older. Even in the later stages of their careers, these offenders averaged only a few thousand dollars per year for their crimes.

Only 25 percent of the group said that they had trouble adjusting to prison life. However, with advancing age and more frequent incarceration, their main source of difficulty was not the other inmates but their own feelings and the growing realization that life is short and the desire to be on the outside living it. The inmates strongly felt that what they needed most upon release was someone who cared and employment. Drugs and alcohol were found to play a prominent role in the offenders' lives. The offenders who had problems handling both had the highest offense rates.

This report is noteworthy for the manner in which it states the policy implications of the research. These conclusions are of particular importance to the criminal justice researcher in that he/she is interested in providing, through research, information upon which policy can be built. With regard to rehabilitation, these inmates felt that prison programs did not provide a strong inducement for them to go straight. They stated that they would prefer job training programs and it was also clear that, by their own admission, they could benefit from drug/alcohol treatment programs. In terms of the deterrent effect of punishment, it was clear that the inmates did not fit the definition of the rational criminal and that they were unconcerned about the possibility of apprehension. Over half the sample said that "nothing" could have deterred their return to crime following release from prison. In fact, those who served longer sentences did not have shorter periods of street crime after release and until the next incarceration.

Finally regarding incapacitation, if it were enacted as a policy, the research indicated that the greatest effect in crime prevention would come from imprisoning the younger, more active offenders, since individual offense rates appeared to decline substantially with age. Unfortunately, it is very difficult, if not impossible, to develop an accurate method of predicting criminal behavior and identifying this crime-prone group.

Limitations of Self-Report Studies

The two examples of self-report studies presented differed in terms of their subject matter but they share in the attempt to uncover unreported crime. The major problem is the determination of validity — How do you know that the respondents are telling you the truth?

In the Gold study, the use of the "criterion group" of youngsters whose offenses were known by the group of informants raises some questions. For example, Pepinsky[37] has stated that Gold's informants made it harder, not easier for him to gauge whether his respondents were telling the truth. Why should the informants be considered any more credible than the respondents? How did Gold know if the informants were telling the truth? The second issue is an ethical one. Did the use of the informants violate Gold's promise to the respondents to maintain the anonymity and confidentiality of their information?

The habitual offender study also presents a number of problems. The first is the paradox of using official records (the "rap sheet") to check the accuracy of the data gathered from questionnaires and interviews. As Nettler has written,[36] it is strange that critics of official records should then use them as a valid indicator of unreported or unknown crime. Even if this technique is an excellent one, the problem of exaggeration still remains. Offenders, in their desire to appear "bad," may have confessed to crimes which they never committed. They may also gain some perverse pleasure out of conning the researcher, thus demonstrating that the inmate, not the researcher, is the true expert on crime.

Conclusions Concerning Self-Report Studies

One of the strongest critics of this method, Nettler[36] has concluded that the examination of the reliability and validity of measures of crime based on confessions of it does not encourage substitution of self-reports for official statistics. Yet, it is apparent that the self-report technique offers the researcher another method of discovering information about crime. As Hirschi and his colleagues[29] have written, the method allows active participation in the research process in a way not possible when the researcher is dependent upon data produced by others (police records, or program officials) and the researcher should recognize the value of such an all-purpose tool is dependent upon the skill with which it is applied to the task at hand.

TRIANGULATION

Triangulation refers to the use of several different research methods to measure a phenomenon.[2] Triangulation is also concerned with convergent-discriminant validation. Using different methods to measure crime (UCR, NCS, self report) should yield the same findings (convergence) while measures of different things with the same measure should yield different results (discrimination). Triangulation thus offers a way to validate the accuracy and reliability of different criminal justice data sources.

For example, a comparison of UCR and NCS data have indicated that they share common strengths and weaknesses as measures of criminality. Hindelang[27] reported that there was a close proximity between UCR data and an earlier victimization study in terms of the frequency in the occurrence of index crimes. However, Booth and his colleagues[5] found substantial differences in the ability of both the UCR and NCS to distinguish between various types of crime and concluded that neither is a satisfactory index of crime for the purpose of explaining the cause of crime. Decker[16] discovered that there were positive correlations between the two data sources with regard to the index offenses and concluded that the "official measures of crime provided a relatively good indicator of the distribution of Part I crimes as measured by victim surveys." On the other hand, a mathematical model constructed by Eck and Riccio[17] to determine the nature and extent of the relationship between UCR and NCS data demonstrated that reported crime counts either exaggerate the amount of change in victimizations or tend to misrepresent the direction of change in victimizations. Finally, Schneider[44] compared and analyzed differences between survey and police data for a set of 212 matched cases from Portland and reported that "differences between survey and police data are generally random rather than systematic errors in the survey data produced by memory decay." Of course, the main problem when attempting to triangulate UCR and NCS data is to obtain data sets from the same jurisdiction, for the same time period which also are concerned with the same crimes. It may be necessary to conduct a victimization survey on a smaller scale within a particular area and then make the comparison to UCR information.

However, triangulation is not limited to a comparison of UCR and NCS results. It can be used any time there are multiple data sources which can be used to measure a phenomenon. For example, Baldus, Pulaski, and Woodworth[3] used triangulation to determine an accurate method to ascertain the proportionality of Georgia's death penalty statute. Their research was based upon the fact that the Georgia State Supreme Court is required by law to conduct a review of all death sentences in order to determine whether the sentence is excessive or disproportionate when compared to the sentence imposed in similar cases, considering both the crime and the defendant. The authors attempted to determine the best method of making this determination. They opted for a triangulation approach using three different methods for identifying similar cases for comparative purposes while cross-checking the results of each method. They utilized the: (1) Salient Factors, (2) Main Determinants and, (3) Index Methods to identify similar cases. The salient factors approach involves the selection of cases based upon the facts and circumstances of the case which is under review. Here, it is the case itself which serves as a basis to identify similar cases. Under the main determinants approach, data are collected on a number of death-eligible cases and then a multivariate statistical analysis is conducted to determine the variables which distinguish those cases sentenced to death versus those which are not. The index method classifies cases in terms of the probability that the defendant will receive a death sentence. An analysis of Georgia cases led to the conclusion that the main determinants (quantitative analysis) method offered the best hope of identifying the factors which influence juries while also determining the pool of cases by matching large numbers of cases on the basis of many variables.[4] In this manner, triangulation can help to solve the reliability and/or validity problem by identifying and considering the use of multiple data sets or multiple methods of measurement.

CONCLUSION

The criminal justice researcher faces serious problems when attempting to measure crime. The validity and reliability of the indicators selected are of paramount concern. This chapter has raised some of the critical issues surrounding the use of the most common sources of crime information (UCR, NCS, and self-report studies). They all have their particular strengths and weaknesses, and it is important to remember that the choice of crime measures can affect both the course and results of the study. Unfortunately, none of these measures is error-free. We must recognize the limitations of each, attempt to deal with them, and in some way attempt to improve them.

KEY TERMS

Convergent-Discriminant Validity
Crime Clock
Crime Rate
Criterion Group
Households Touched by Crime
Index Crimes
National Crime Survey
Reliability
Self-Report Method
Triangulation
Uniform Crime Reports
Validity

STUDY GUIDE

1. What is the definition of validity and how does it apply to the indicators discussed in this chapter? Perform the same exercise with reliability.

2. Read the following hypothetical example[20] and describe how it would be classified in the *Uniform Crime Reports* and under the *National Crime Survey*. What would the differences be and how well would the classification describe what actually happened?

A young couple living in the household of the young woman's parents in Stanford, Connecticut, go to New York City on December 31 to celebrate New Year's Eve. They park their car in a lot on the east side of Manhattan and have a leisurely dinner at a nearby restaurant.

After dinner when they return to their car, they are accosted by five young males just outside the parking lot and are taken into an adjacent alley way, at approximately 11:00 P.M.

One of the youths threatens the couple with a revolver, and the other four take turns raping the woman. When the woman resists, one of the youths assaults her with a knife, and then he also assaults the man.

Following the acts of rape, the youths take the woman's purse and the man's wallet and they appear to flee.

It is now 1:00 A.M., January 1. The couple have to travel several blocks to report the incident to the police. When they finally return to the parking lot with a police officer at 3:00 A.M., they discover that their automobile is missing.

A week later, three young males are stopped by the police in Newark, N.J., driving the couple's car through a red stoplight and they are arrested.

REFERENCES

1. Black, Donald: The production of crime rates. *American Sociological Review,* 35: 733-748, 1970.
2. Babbie, Earl: *The Practice of Social Research.* Belmont, CA: Wadsworth, 1983.
3. Baldus, David C., Pulaski, Charles, and Woodworth, George: Comparative review of death sentences: An empirical study of the Georgia experience. *Journal of Criminal Law and Criminology,* 74: 661-753.
4. Baldus, David C., Pulaski, Charles A. Jr., Woodworth, George, and Kyle, Frederick D.: Identifying comparatively excessive sentences of death: A quantitative approach. *Stanford Law Review,* 33: 1-76.
5. Booth, Alan, Johnson, David R., and Choldin, Harvey M.: Correlates of city crime rates: victimization surveys versus official statistics. *Social Problems,* 25: 187-197, 1977.

6. Bureau of Justice Statistics Bulletin: *Criminal Victimization 1983*. Washington, D.C.: U.S. Department of Justice, June, 1984.

7. Bureau of Justice Statistics Bulletin: *Households Touched by Crime, 1982*. Washington, D.C.: U.S. Department of Justice, 1983.

8. Bureau of Justice Statistics Bulletin: *Households Touched by Crime, 1983*. Washington, D.C.: U.S. Department of Justice, 1984.

9. Bureau of Justice Statistics Bulletin: *Households Touched by Crime, 1984*. Washington, D.C.: U.S. Department of Justice, 1985.

10. Bureau of Justice Statistics Bulletin: *Measuring Crime*. Washington, D.C.: U.S. Department of Justice, February, 1981.

11. Bureau of Justice Statistics Bulletin: *The Prevalence of Crime*. Washington, D.C.: U.S. Department of Justice, March, 1981.

12. Bureau of Justice Statistics: *Criminal Victimization in the United States, 1982*. Washington, D.C.: U.S. Department of Justice, 1984.

13. Bureau of Justice Statistics: *Criminal Victimization in the United States, 1983*. Washington, D.C.: U.S. Department of Justice, 1985.

14. Bureau of Justice Statistics: *Report to the Nation on Crime and Justice: The Data*. Washington, D.C.: U.S. Department of Justice, 1983.

15. Cook, Thomas D. and Campbell, Donald T.: *Quasi-Experimentation: Design and Analysis Issues for Field Settings*. Boston: Houghton Mifflin, 1979.

16. Decker, Scott H.: Official crime rates and victim surveys: An empirical comparison. *Journal of Criminal Justice, 5*: 47-54, 1977.

17. Eck, J. Ernst and Riccio, Lucius J.: Relationship between reported crime rates and victimization survey results: an empirical and analytical study. *Journal of Criminal Justice, 7*: 293-308, 1979.

18. Federal Bureau of Investigation: *Uniform Crime Reports for the United States*. Washington, D.C.: U.S. Department of Justice, 1984.

19. Ferracuti, Franco, Hernandez, Rosita Perez, and Wolfgang, Marvin E.: A study of police errors in crime classification. *Journal of Criminal Law, Criminology and Police Science, 53*: 113-119, 1962.

20. Fienberg, Stephen E.: Victimization and the national crime survey: Problems of design and analysis. In Feinberg, S.E. and Reiss, A.J. Jr. (Eds.): *Indicators of Crime and Criminal Justice: Quantitative Studies*. Washington D.C.: U.S. Government Printing Office, 1980, pp. 33-40.

21. Garofalo, James and Hindelang, Michael J.: *An Introduction to the National Crime Survey*. Washington, D.C.: U.S. Department of Justice, 1977.

22. Gold, Martin: Undetected criminal behavior. *Journal of Research in Crime and Delinquency, 3*: 27-46, 1966.

23. Gottfredson, Don M. and Gottfredson, Michael R.: Data for criminal justice evaluation: Some resources and pitfalls. In Klein, M.W. and Teilmann, K.S. (Eds.): *Handbook of Criminal Justice Evaluation*. Beverly Hills, CA: Sage, 1980, pp. 97-118.

24. Gottfredson, Michael R. and Hindelang, Michael J.: A consideration of telescoping and memory decay biases in victimization surveys. *Journal of Criminal Justice, 5*: 205-216, 1977.

25. Hagan, Frank E.: *Research Methods in Criminal Justice and Criminology*. New York, Macmillan, 1982.

26. Hardt, Robert H., and Peterson-Hardt, Sandra: Self-reporting of delinquency. *Journal of Research in Crime and Delinquency,* 14: 247-261, 1977.

27. Hindelang, Michael J.: The uniform crime reports revisited. *Journal of Criminal Justice,* 2: 1-17, 1974.

28. Hindelang, Michael J., Hirschi, Travis, and Weis, Joseph G.: *Measuring Delinquency.* Beverly Hills, CA, Sage, 1981.

29. Hirschi, Travis, Hindelang, Michael J., and Weis, Joseph G.: The status of self-report measures. In Klein, M.W. and Teilmann, K.S. (Eds.): *Handbook of Criminal Justice Evaluation.* Beverly Hills, CA, Sage, 1980, pp. 473-488.

30. Johnson, Kirk Alan, and Wasielewski, Patricia L.: A commentary on victimization research and the importance of meaning structures. *Criminology,* 20: 205-222, 1982.

31. Kleinman, Paula Holzman and Lukoff, Irving Faber: Official crime data: Lag in recording time as a threat to validity. *Criminology,* 19: 449-454, 1981.

32. Laub, John H.: Ecological considerations in victim reporting to the police. *Journal of Criminal Justice,* 9: 419-430, 1981.

33. Levine, James P., Musheno, Michael C., and Palumbo, Denis J.: *Criminal Justice: A Public Policy Approach.* New York: Harcourt Brace Jovanovitch, 1980.

34. Levine, James P.: The potential for crime overreporting in criminal victimization surveys. *Criminology,* 14: 307-330, 1976.

35. McClintock, F.H.: The dark figure of crime. In Radzinowicz, L. and Wolfgang, M.E. (Eds.): *Crime and Justice, Volume I: The Criminal in Society.* New York: Basic Books, 1977, pp. 126-139.

36. Nettler, Gwynn: *Explaining Crime.* New York: McGraw-Hill, 1984.

37. Pepinsky, Harold E.: *Crime Control Strategies: An Introduction to the Study of Crime.* New York: Oxford University Press, 1980.

38. Petersilia, Joan, Greenwood, Peter W., and Lavin, Marvin: *Criminal Careers of Habitual Felons.* Santa Monica, CA: Rand Corporation, 1977.

39. Petersilia, Joan: Validity of criminality data derived from personal interviews. In Wellford, C. (Ed.): *Quantitative Studies in Criminology.* Beverly Hills, CA: Sage, 1978, pp. 30-47.

40. Quinney, Richard: What do crime rates mean? In Radzinowicz, L. and Wolfgang, M.E. (Eds.): *Crime and Justice, Volume I: The Criminal in Society.* New York: Basic Books, 1977, pp. 107-111.

41. Reid, Sue Titus: *Crime and Criminology.* New York: Holt, Rinehart and Winston, 1979.

42. Reiss, Albert J., Jr.: Understanding changes in crime rates. In Fienberg, S.E. and Reiss, A.J., Jr. (Eds.): *Indicators of Crime and Criminal Justice: Quantitative Studies.* Washington, D.C.: U.S. Government Printing Office, 1980, pp. 11-17.

43. Savitz, Leonard D.: Official police statistics and their limitations. In Savitz, L.D. and Johnston, N. (Eds.): *Crime in Society.* New York: John Wiley and Sons, 1978, pp. 69-81.

44. Schneider, Anne L.: Differences between survey and police information about crime. In Lehnen, R.G. and Skogan, W.G. (Eds.): *The National Crime Survey: Working Papers, Volume I: Current and Historical Perspectives.* Washington, D.C.: U.S. Government Printing Office, 1981, pp. 39-46.

45. Schneider, Anne R. and Sumi, David: Patterns of forgetting and telescoping:

An analysis of LEAA survey victimization data. *Criminology,* 19: 400-410, 1981.

46. Seidman, David and Couzens, Michael: Getting the crime rate down: Political pressures and crime reporting. *Law and Society Review,* 8: 456-493, 1974.

47. Sellin, Thorsten: The significance of records of crime. In Radzinowicz, L. and Wolfgang, M.E. (Eds.): *Crime and Justice, Volume 1: The Criminal in Society.* New York: Basic Books, 1971, pp. 121-129.

48. Sheley, Joseph F.: *Understanding Crime: Concepts, Issues, Decisions.* Belmont, CA: Wadsworth, 1979.

49. Skogan, Wesley G.: Citizen reporting of crime: Some national panel data. *Criminology,* 13: 535-549, 1976.

50. Skogan, Wesley G.: The 'dark figure' of unreported crime. *Crime and Delinquency,* 23: 41-50, 1977.

51. Skogan, Wesley G.: *Issues in the Measurement of Victimization.* Washington, D.C.: U.S. Government Printing Office, 1981.

52. Skogan, Wesley G.: Measurement problems in official and survey crime rates. *Journal of Criminal Justice,* 3: 17-31, 1975.

53. Skogan, Wesley G.: *Victimization Surveys and Criminal Justice Planning.* Washington, D.C.: National Institute of Law Enforcement and Criminal Justice, 1978.

54. Sparks, Richard: Using national data. *In Final Report, UPR/NPR Seminar: National Reporting in the 1980s.* San Francisco: National Council on Crime and Delinquency, 1982, pp. 8-13.

55. Wheeler, Stanton: Criminal statistics: A reformulation of the problem. *Journal of Criminal Law, Criminology and Police Science,* 58: 317-324, 1967.

56. Wilkins, Leslie T.: *Evaluation of Penal Measures.* New York: Random House, 1969.

57. Wolfgang, Marvin E.: Uniform crime reports: A critical appraisal. *University of Pennsylvania Law Review,* 3: 708-738, 1963.

58. Zolbe, Paul A.: The role of the uniform crime reporting program as a data source for criminological research: Promise and limitations. Paper presented at the Annual Meeting of the American Society of Criminology, Washington, D.C., 1981.

CHAPTER FIVE

LIBRARY RESEARCH
IN CRIMINAL JUSTICE

THE RESEARCH process begins with an idea or some curiosity on the part of the researcher. However, a great deal of work must transpire before an idea is translated into an actual research project. A portion of this preparatory work is the careful review of existing information about the topic. This review of existing information on a topic may not seem as exciting as actually designing the research methodology or collecting the data. This review is, however, the most critical part of the research process. The information collected in this review guides all other phases of the research project from design of the methodology to writing the final research report or article. This search for topical material is called a **review of the literature.** It is critical to any specific research project and to the scientific research process. It is through this review of the literature that the cumulative development as well as the careful replication of scientific information is accomplished.

When a researcher conducts a review of the literature she or he is attempting to gather information that other researchers have developed on the specific topic(s) of interest. This is a valuable tool for the researcher. This review of the literature gives the researcher information about:

1. The amount and type of information which exists on a specific topic;
2. How other researchers have defined concepts related to a specific topic;
3. What hypotheses were developed;
4. What methodologies and operationalizations of variables were used to study the topic;
5. What subjects were studied, in what places and at what times;

6. Any difficulties or problems that might have been encountered by previous researchers;
7. What ethical problems were present in prior research; and
8. What impact or influence the research has had on the scientific community as well as society in general.

During a review of the literature, a researcher does not simply read the previous research and accept the findings and conclusions as fact. A review of the literature is a critical appraisal of the strengths and weaknesses of these studies. The researcher wants to conduct a study that will not only build upon existing information but will also improve the quality of knowledge within a specific substantive area.

LIBRARY RESOURCES

Most reviews of the literature begin with the library. Libraries at various institutions and organizations contain a wealth of information and a number of information gathering resources. Some libraries are more specialized, such as the library of the National Institute of Corrections. Others are more general, such as university libraries.

There are a number of places to begin a search for information in a library. The one most familiar to most library users is the card catalog. The card catalog contains information about most of the books in the library. Card catalogs index books in three ways: by author, subject, and title. In each of these three sections of the card catalog the cards on each particular book are filed alphabetically by either author, subject, or title. The cards on each book contain at a minimum the title, author, edition, publisher, and publication date. This card also contains the book's call number. These call numbers are based on one of two standard classification systems used by every library. These are the Dewey Decimal Classification System and the Library of Congress Classification System. These classification systems specify the location of a book in the library. To find a book you must have the card catalog number. Books in the area of criminal justice and criminology are identified by the prefix HV and the numbers 340 to 360.

Many times a book which is not contained in the collection of a library may be needed. In this instance it is possible to obtain a book through the interlibrary loan service provided at most libraries. This service allows the library user to request a book on loan from another library. It is a useful service but it may take some time to receive the book and these books are not generally renewable.

While the card catalog may contain a number of references, books do not always contain the most current information available on a given topic. The most current information is usually available in periodicals or professional journals. Articles from these sources are found through a number of indexes available at most libraries. However, not all indexes list articles in all existing publications.

One of the most widely known indexes is the *Readers Guide to Periodical Literature* This index contains an alphabetical subject/author index of popular periodicals published in the United States. These periodicals are those such as *Time, Newsweek,* and *U.S. News and World Report.* The articles in these periodicals are prepared for the general public. They are not as scholarly or detailed as those articles published in professional journals. Researchers may review some of these articles in an effort to survey the popular literature on a topic. However, they are not a primary source of a review of the literature.

Abstracting indexes are more specialized than *Readers Guide* and also contain information on articles in professional journals. Abstracting indexes contain author and subject indexes. An added benefit to the researcher is that these indexes also contain a condensed summary or abstract of the publication. It is possible to then determine if the article will be useful without going to the specific publication and reading the article. Those abstracting indexes of particular interest to criminal justice and criminology researchers are:

> *Abstracts on Criminology and Penology*
> *Criminal Justice Abstracts*
> *Criminal Justice Periodical Index*
> *Index to Abstracts on Crime and Juvenile Delinquency 1968-1975*
> *Index-Abstracts of Research in the Bureau of Prisons 1976-77*
> *Police Science Abstracts*
> *Applied Science and Technology Index*
> *Current Law Index*
> *Index to Legal Periodicals*
> *Psychological Abstracts*
> *Sage Public Administration Abstracts*
> *Social Science Index*
> *Social Work Research and Abstracts*
> *Sociological Abstracts*[1]

Other more specialized abstracting indexes are also available and are of use when the researcher is interested in a more specific substantive area. Most of the indexes are published annually. The usual practice is to look for publications over the last five to ten years when conducting a review of the literature. The time frame for the search will depend on the topic and nature of the research project.

In addition to the abstracting indexes, a number of topical bibliographies are available. Each of these bibliographers describe references dealing with a specific substantive area. For example, *Basic Selected Bibliography of Crime and Delinquency,*[2] *Criminal Justice Bibliography,*[3] and *Criminology, Law Enforcement and Offender Treatment*[4] are worthwhile sources of information. O'Block[1] lists a number of these bibliographies. However, attention must be paid to the publication dates of these bibliographies. The more recent the date of publication, the more recent the references contained in the bibliography and/or the more lengthy the time frame covered by the bibliography.

In addition to specialized bibliographies and abstracts, libraries also contain a number of general and specialized dictionaries, encyclopedias, annuals and yearbooks which can provide a wealth of information. In addition to these references, newspapers may also provide information not found in more scholarly texts. Most newspaper literature is stored on microfilm. *Newsbank* indexes 190 newspapers from 103 cities. Articles may be identified and selected using subject headings in 12 categories. One of these categories is "Law and Order" and contains articles under a variety of subject sub-headings such as: correctional facilities, crime rates, judges, police, and victimless crime.

When using newspaper articles, the opinion must be separated from the facts. Articles must be carefully screened to separate the verified facts from opinions. However, as a source of up-to-date information on current events, the newspaper can be extremely valuable.

Computerized Bibliographic Searches

A number of libraries are equipped to provide the capability for researchers to conduct a computer search of abstracts contained in indexes. The computer search is an efficient and swift way to identify sources for a review of literature. Most computer searches access databases containing information on a general topical area. Key words identifying the specific area of interest are entered into the computer. The program then searches the general topical file or database for references containing or indexed under the key words.

Obviously, the initial task in conducting a computer search is to identify the database. One database of specific interest to criminal justice researchers is the National Criminal Justice Reference Service (NCJRS) database which contains information on a broad spectrum of criminal justice topics. This database indexes a wide variety of government documents, reports, published papers, books, and articles from 1972 to the present.

Another database of special relevances is the *Criminal Justice Periodical Index*. This index includes 120 administration of justice and law enforcement periodicals and journals from 1975 to the present. Other related databases include: *Child Abuse and Neglect, DRUG INFO and Alcohol Use and Abuse, Sociological Abstracts, Mental Health Abstracts, Psycinfo* (Psychological Abstracts), and *Social Science Index*. Obviously, not all libraries will have all computerized databases. When a database is available, the greater the amount of information contained in a database, the greater the output from the computerized search.

Some libraries pay a portion of the costs for these searches. However, the user will also be responsible for part of the cost. The more complex the search and the more database accessed for the search, the greater the cost. The fees are reasonable given the time this form of search can save a researcher. These computer searches are also cost effective in that the databases are generally more current than published abstracts or indexes.

National Institute of Justice/NCJRS

The National Institute of Justice (NIJ) publishes numerous government documents. This federal agency provides a number of sources of information and reference services. The National Criminal Justice Reference Service (NCJRS), sponsored by the National Institute of Justice, was established in 1972 as a means to disseminate criminal justice information. The NCJRS operates a number of clearinghouses and information centers. It also distributes information from the Bureau of Justice Statistics (BJS) through the Justice Statistics Clearinghouse. This reference service offers a number of information sources. The NCJRS maintains a library with a large collection of documents which it makes available to libraries through an interlibrary loan service at a nominal fee to cover postage and handling.

The NCJRS also supports an online database collection of abstracts of books, articles, and other unpublished papers and reports covering the full range of criminal justice substantive areas. A Document Retrieval

Index is available on microfiche. Researchers may purchase this bibliographical information on the holdings of the NCJRS library collection and database. Supplements are produced annually so that the index can be constantly updated.

The NCJRS will also conduct specialized database searches at the request of researchers. These are conducted for a fee and can be specified to meet the unique needs of any research project. The NCJRS also produces Topical Searches and Topical Bibliographies covering substantive criminal justice areas. These offer an overview of the literature in a given topical area. The Topical Searches cover a broad range of topics in Corrections, Courts, Criminology, Police, Victims, Crime Prevention, Juvenile Justice, and Dispute Resolution. The Topical Bibliographies contain a more detailed list of references on criminal justice topics. Both the searches and bibliographies are constantly updated and revised to reflect new information and topics of interest in criminal justice.

The NCJRS also operates two clearinghouses, the Juvenile Justice Clearinghouse and the Justice Statistics Clearinghouse. Researchers may register with these clearinghouses and receive a copy of *NIJ Reports,* a journal containing abstracts of selected documents, information about upcoming meetings, and listings of new products and services. Both the Juvenile Justice and Justice Statistics Clearinghouses can put researchers in contact with information specialists who can assist in identifying resources. These clearinghouses can also provide copies of bulletins produced by the National Institute of Justice on various topics related to juvenile and criminal justice.

The NCJRS and each clearinghouse can be contacted by mail or toll free numbers. The addresses and phone numbers are listed below.

National Institute of Justice/NCJRS
Box 6000
Rockville, MD 20850
(800) 851-3420

Juvenile Justice Clearinghouse/NCJRS
Box 6000
Rockville, MD 20850
(800) 638-8736

Justice Statistics Clearinghouse/NCJRS
Box 6000
Rockville, MD 20850
(800) 732-3277

NATIONAL INSTITUTE OF CORRECTIONS INFORMATION CENTER

The National Institute of Corrections operates an Information Center which serves as the national clearinghouse for the collection, preparation, and dissemination of information on adult corrections. The NIC Information Center staff provides assistance on a broad range of topics in adult corrections. Materials from the NIC library collection of over 10,000 volumes are accessible as well as computerized information searches to supplement library materials.

The phone number and address of the NIC Information are listed below.

NIC Information Center
1790 30th Street
Suite 130
Boulder, CO 80301
(303) 444-1101

These national clearinghouses are invaluable sources of information for researchers. They can provide up to date information that is not available from libraries. Additionally, the resource personnel at these clearinghouses can provide referrals to other agencies on individuals who may provide additional information.

CRIMINAL JUSTICE STATISTICS

Researchers have available a number of sources for statistics. Some of these statistics are official statistics, that is, "data gathered by agencies on clients coming into contact with the agency" (Irving, 1983: 259) or data gathered on information officially reported to and retained by the agency. The Uniform Crime Report published by the FBI is the most widely known official source of statistics. This publication contains information on offenses reported to police personnel from most police jurisdictions across the United States (see Chapter Four).

Many other national, regional, and state criminal justice agencies produce official data. An excellent resource for various official and survey criminal justice statistics is the *Sourcebook for Criminal Justice Statistics* published annually by the U.S. Department of Justice, Bureau of Justice Statistics. The data are national data and, "where possible they are displayed by regions, state, and cities to increase their value for local decisionmakers and for comparative analyses."[5]

The book is organized into six sections: Characteristics of the Criminal Justice Systems, Public Attitudes Toward Crime and Criminal Justice-related Topics, Nature and Distribution of Known Offenses, Characteristics and Distribution of Persons Arrested, Judicial Processing of Defendants, and Persons Under Correctional Supervision. Each section contains tables with the specific statistical information. Data on juveniles and the juvenile justice system are also available in some sections. The *Sourcebook* is valuable because it contains a summary of data from a number of sources. Therefore, time and effort on the part of the researcher in locating these statistics may be saved.

Other statistics are also available from the Bureau of Justice Statistics of the U.S. Department of Justice. The Bureau of Justice Statistics produces data from a number of sources. Reports from the National Crime Survey, a survey of criminal victimization in the United States are the basis for a number of general reports of annual victimization trends as well as reports on specialized forms of victimization such as victimization of the elderly, violent crime by strangers, family violence, and the economic costs of victimization (see Chapter Four).

The Bureau of Justice Statistics also produces reports on Corrections such as, reports on annual prison admissions and releases, time served in prison, capital punishment, and jail inmates. Other reports on topics within the area of Probation and Parole, Courts, and Privacy and Security are also available.

OFFENDER BASED TRACKING SYSTEM

Data such as those discussed in the previous section have been criticized as being "analytic rather than systemic; i.e., the data reveal information on separate parts of the criminal justice system rather than on the system as an integrated process . . ."[6] These data present information about each component of the system: police, courts, corrections, but cannot provide data on how the processes and procedures of one unit impact other units in the system. Nor can they provide tracking information concerning the criminal justice system processing from point of entry (police) to point of exit (parole). Additionally, longitudinal data concerning this processing is unavailable when the data are retained as distinct component-specific data.

An excellent example of longitudinal, systemic data is the Offender-Based Tracking System (OBTS). An offender-based tracking system is a means of following offenders as they are processed through the various stages and components of the criminal justice system. For example, OBTS can track an offender from arrest (police) to trial (courts) to incarceration (corrections). Since the system is based on offenders, it is possible to follow the cycles of processing of individual offenders who enter the system, exit in some fashion, and then return. Consequently, repeat offenders may be identified and tracked as they subsequently return with new convictions.

It is possible with OBTS to follow groups of offenders as well. This is probably the real advantage of OBTS, that is, aggregate data on groups of offenders. For example, a cohort of offenders entering the system (arrest) at a given time period may be followed through the processes of the criminal justice system. Similarly, a group of offenders arrested for a similar offense such as burglary, may be tracked through the stages of criminal justice system processing. These tracking capabilities can provide valuable information for researchers and policy makers. The advantages of an offender-based tracking system are:

1. OBTS can demonstrate how and how many individuals leave the criminal justice system at various stages in the criminal justice process.
2. OBTS can provide data on the amount of time it takes to process individuals through stages in the criminal justice system.
3. OBTS can provide data on sentence disparity.
4. OBTS can provide rates/probabilities related to conviction and incarceration which can be utilized to predict how many offenders will "flow" through the various points in the system.
5. Most importantly, OBTS can provide a systemic perspective on criminal justice and can provide systemic data to policymakers and researchers.[7]

An Offender Based Tracking System can produce data that is extremely valuable to both scholars and practitioners. For example, through the use of OBTS data all felony arrests for a given year can be tracked to determine the probability of conviction and incarceration for specific crimes. This is extremely important in attempts to predict prison populations. OBTS data can also be used to examine the impact of legal and extra legal factors such as race on the probability of conviction and/or incarceration.

The development of an Offender Based Tracking System is a lengthy and often political process. It requires that agencies of the criminal justice system coordinate their data collection and retention. It requires time to overcome the longstanding territoriality of the separate agencies and the resulting hesitance to share information. Similarly, problems may develop from limited automation of criminal justice agencies which makes the data collection and sharing more time consuming and costly. However, with planning, time, money, and effort, a data base with the combined information necessary for an OBTS can be developed and maintained.

CONCLUSION

The research process begins with an idea. This idea must be brought to fruition through a review of the literature. This review gives direction and substance to the research project.

A number of sources of data for the literature review and research can be garnered from libraries and reference services. An especially valuable source of data for system processing information is the Offender Based Tracking System (OBTS).

KEY TERMS

Review of the literature
Card catalog
Readers Guide to Periodical Literature
Abstracting indexes
Topical bibliographies
Newsbank
Computerized bibliographic searches
National Criminal Justice Reference Service
NIJ Reports
NIC Information Center
Sourcebook for Criminal Justice Statistics
Bureau of Justice Statistics
Offender Based Tracking System

STUDY GUIDE

1. What is the purpose of a review of the literature? What questions can it answer?

2. What is the purpose of a card catalog?
3. How are the *Readers Guide to Periodical Literature,* abstracting indexes, and topical bibliographies different from one another?
4. What are the benefits of computerized bibliographic searches?
5. What is the National Criminal Justice Reference Service? What can it provide for a researcher?
6. Describe the sources available to researchers who want to obtain existing statistical information.
7. What is an Offender Based Tracking System?
8. What are the benefits of an Offender Based Tracking System?

REFERENCES

1. O'Block, Robert L. *Criminal Justice Research Sources,* 2nd Ed. (Cincinnati: Anderson, 1986).
2. David, P.R. (Ed.) *Basic Selected Bibliography of Crime and Delinquency,* (Albuquerque, New Mexico: University of New Mexico, Institute for Social Research and Development, 1971).
3. Marcus, Marvin. *Criminal Justice Bibliography* (Georgia State University, School of Urban Life, 1976).
4. Kinton, Jack F. *Criminology, Law Enforcement and Offender Treatment* (Aurora, Illinois: Social Science and Sociological Resources, 1974).
5. *Sourcebook of Criminal Justice Statistics — 1985.* (U.S. Department of Justice, Bureau of Justice Statistics, 1986).
6. Irving, Richard. "Assessing United States Criminal Justice Statistics Information: An Introduction and Selected List of Bibliographic Sources," *Reference Quarterly.* Spring (1983). 257-265.
7. *Tracking the Offender* (Kentucky Criminal Justice Statistical Analysis Center, March 1986).

CHAPTER SIX

ELEMENTS OF RESEARCH DESIGN

IN THIS chapter, we will introduce the student to the main elements of research design. Research design is nothing more than the plan, blueprint or recipe for the proposed study. It designates the manner in which the variables and objects under study will be compared and analyzed. It outlines the strategy of the investigation in order to obtain answers to research questions. The ultimate purpose of the research design is to insure that any conclusions drawn from the research are the result of the interaction between the objects under study and not due to the manner in which the research was conducted. The design should indicate how variables will be measured, how to obtain the information, and how the final analysis will be conducted. Therefore, statistical analysis does not come into play until after the design has been executed. However, the research design anticipates the type of statistical analysis which will be utilized (see Chapter Two). With this introduction in mind, let us review the basic types of research design.

THE CLASSICAL EXPERIMENT

The classical experiment has been termed "the Cadillac" of research designs[12] because it is so powerful. By powerful, we mean that the classical experiment has the ability to screen out undesirable influences upon the research. The results of the experiment are held to be valid because any alternative explanations have been held constant.

The classical experiment has been traditionally defined as research in which one or more variables are manipulated by the experimenter under carefully controlled conditions.[3] Unfortunately, the criminal justice researcher seldom conducts his/her research under laboratory conditions,

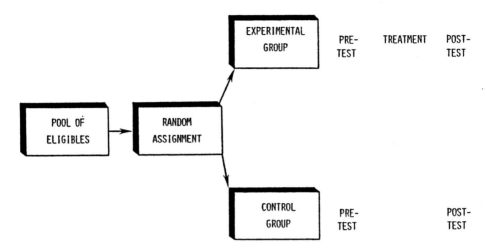

FIGURE 6-1: The Classical Experiment.

but the classical experiment is important because it serves as the basis for all other types of research designs. For example, the classical experiment examines if a causal connection exists between the variables under consideration. Thus, it examines the effect of the independent variable (usually designated as X) upon the dependent variable (Y). The design involves a comparison between groups of individuals or variables. Figure 6-1 presents a diagram of the classical experiment.

The key feature of the classical experiment is randomization. Randomization means that each element (i.e., individual) has an equal chance of being assigned to the experimental group and that the selection of one individual does not affect the chance that any other individual will be selected. Random assignment insures that the experimental and control groups are comparable. Therefore, any outcome which presents itself can be assumed to be a legitimate effect of the treatment and not due to inherent differences between the experimental and control groups.

First, let us define what we mean by treatment. In the field of criminal justice, the treatment can take a number of forms, depending upon the nature of the study. For example, the treatment could be a special form of police foot patrolling, an habitual offender law, or a halfway house program. The elements of the study could be neighborhoods, sentenced offenders, or probationers or parolees. Put simply, the research design usually begins with a group of "eligibles": elements which (due to some criminological theory) are presumed to be amenable to the proposed "treatment."[4]

These eligibles are then assigned, through randomization, to the experimental or control group. Another possible method is termed matching. Here, quota sampling (see Chapter Seven) to construct a matrix of individuals who possess certain characteristics which are of importance to the study. Then, random assignment is used to place subjects in the experimental and control groups. The two groups should be equal with regard to your important variables. Yet, one of the basic problems with matching is that the equivalence of experimental and control groups is limited to those variables which were used as the basis for the match (i.e., race, prior record, education). It could always be argued that the results of the study are due to "unmatched" variables rather than the treatment.[9] For this reason, matching is preferred only when random assignment is impossible.

Next, a pre-test on the dependent variable is then taken before the treatment (independent variable) is administered to the experimental group. Due to random selection, the experimental and control groups are similar or identical in make-up. The only difference between the two groups is the one which the experimenter desires — the experimental group is exposed to the treatment but the control group is not. Any difference between the two groups on the post-test (dependent variable) is presumed to be the result of the treatment. In sum, the classical experiment measures the effectiveness of a treatment by applying it to the experimental group while withholding it from the identical control group and then measuring what happens. Usually, it is assumed that, if there is a treatment effect, it will appear in the outcome of the experimental group but not in the control group. Of course, the selection of a control group is vital to the process of experimentation. Without a control group, we would have no basis of comparison to determine the effect of the treatment.

Farrington has demonstrated that the use of the classical experiment in criminal justice research has been widespread.[9] To demonstrate how the classical experiment can be applied in criminal justice research, let us review one example — the Provo Experiment.

Classical Experiment Example: The Provo Experiment

The Provo Experiment was designed to treat delinquents through the establishment of a social climate which would give these boys the opportunity to experience alternatives to delinquent behavior. The boys would also be given the opportunity to declare publicly their belief (or disbelief)

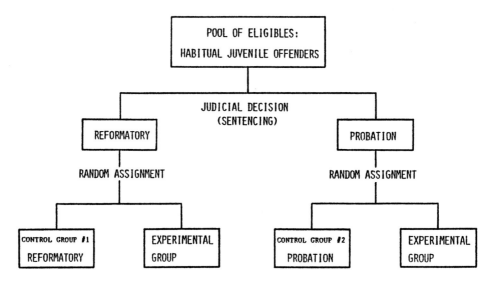

FIGURE 6-2. Original Design of the Provo Experiment.

that they could benefit from a change in values. Basically, the treatment (which was established in 1956) was a "halfway house" (Pinehills) where boys would spend a part of each day. They still lived at home and were otherwise free in the community. According to Empey and Rabow,[8] Pinehills offered a treatment interaction which placed major responsibilities upon peer group decision-making and granted status and recognition to individuals, not only for their own successful participation in the program, but for their willingness to help others. It was specifically designed to help those habitual delinquents "whose persistence made them candidates for the reformatory."

Therefore, the pool of "eligibles" for the Provo Experiment included boys, aged 15-17, who were identified as habitual offenders. Highly disturbed, psychotic boys were not assigned to the program and no more than 20 boys were assigned at one time.

Figure 6-2 outlines the original research design for the Provo Experiment. The initial design was constructed with the idea that all the groups could be drawn randomly from a common population of habitual offenders in Utah county (pool of eligibles). The design would provide a means by which two groups of boys who receive the treatment (experimental group) would be compared to boys in two control groups: (1) a control group of offenders who were placed on probation at the time of sentencing and (2) a control group of boys who were sentenced to the Utah State Industrial School.

The key issue here was to utilize random assignment while not interfering with the judicial process. The judge was instructed to hear the case and make a sentencing decision (probation or incarceration) as though Pinehills did not exist. Thus, the experiment did not interfere with the usual operations of the juvenile court. Then, using random assignment, boys would be selected for the experimental or control groups (Reformatory or Probation). Empey and Rabow[8] have written that this procedure was adopted by the judge with the idea that "in the long run, his contributions to the research would enable judicial decisions to be based ultimately on a more realistic evaluation of treatment programs available" (see also Wood[20]).

However, as is typically the case with criminal justice research (see Finckenauer[10]), the classical experiment proved difficult to implement. First of all, habitual offenders comprised only 15 percent of all cases which came before the court. Thus, the pool of eligibles was not always large enough to fill one experimental and two control groups. Second, Judge Paxman was never inclined to send boys to the reformatory, so that control group was not adequately filled. Therefore, it became necessary to select a random sample of boys from the reformatory and to determine if (and on what characteristics) they differed from the established experimental and control groups. This adjustment was made and no significant difference between groups was revealed. Thus, as we shall see, the Provo Experiment was actually a combination of an experimental and a quasi-experimental design.

Research on the Provo Experiment was conducted and the following results were reported. The measure of recidivism used in the study was the filing of an arrest report six months after release. In the experimental group, it was discovered that 73 percent of the boys assigned to and 84 percent of the boys who had completed Pinehills had not been arrested. None of the experimental group recidivists had been incarcerated. For the probation control group, the success rate for boys who were assigned to regular probation was 73 percent and 77 percent for those who had completed probation. Therefore, the difference in outcome between the experimental and probation control groups was not substantial. Empey and Rabow[8] reported that this lack of results may have been due to the fact that the probation department and the community adopted a daily work program and other facilities as aids to the experiment and the probation department. Finally, the second control group of incarcerated offenders (selected from the reformatory) generated a 58 percent rearrest rate. Half of the incarcerated recidivists had been arrested two or more times during the six month period. Although the classical experimental design broke down for this group, it must be remembered that a comparison of all the groups indicated that they were substantially similar.

However, the weakness here (as we shall see) is that when random assignment is impossible and other measures are used to construct a control group, the groups may differ on attributes which the experimenter is unable to measure and check for. With random assignment, this is not a problem. As Kerlinger[13] has indicated, with random selection, every member of the population has an equal chance of being selected, therefore, members with certain distinguishing characteristics (i.e. they are more "crime prone") will, if selected, probably be counterbalanced in the long run by the selection of other members with the "opposite" quality. Despite its power, however, there are several problems with the use of an experimental design.

Problems in the Use of a Classical Experiment

Ethical and legal issues, raised by Baunach[4] surround the use of the classical experiment in criminal justice research (see Chapter Three). For example, the use of a control group implies that some persons (perhaps offenders) will be deprived of the presumed benefits of a program. Of course, the catch here is that, without sound research, the benefits of a program cannot be accurately ascertained. As Baunach[4] has pointed out, this problem is not insurmountable. If the benefits of the program (treatment) are unknown, the control group offenders are not being deprived. Once the effectiveness of the program is determined, control group offenders can be admitted.

Second, the classical experiment has the potential to encroach upon the decision-making authority of criminal justice agents. The clear solution here, as the Provo Experiment indicated, is to use random assignment after a decision is made. Surely, experimenters cannot expect to randomly sentence people to prison or probation. Modifications can be adopted which do not restrict the power of the classical experimental design while protecting the rights of individuals.

Finally, legal restrictions, such as the National Research Act (1974), have been developed to protect the rights of human subjects. This Act requires that researchers obtain informed and voluntary consent from prisoners. They must be appraised of the risks and benefits to themselves and society as a result of the research. Here, random assignment may be viewed as "arbitrary and capricious" and must be addressed by the experimenter.

However, even if the classical experiment is successfully implemented, several threats to the validity of the research findings still exist which must be anticipated by the researcher. It is important to note that these validity problems can plague all types of research designs, not just the classical experiment.

THREATS TO INTERNAL VALIDITY

Internal validity refers to ways in which the process of experimentation may effect the research results. In other words, the researcher is then uncertain if the outcomes generated by the research are a result of the treatment or the way in which the experiment was conducted. In effect, the experiment becomes a treatment in itself.

Campbell and Stanley[5] identified eight sources of internal validity:

1. **History,** events, in addition to the treatment, may occur between the pre and post tests which are beyond the control of the experimenter. For example, Vito, Longmire, and Kenney[17] reported that, during their evaluation of a police burglary suppression program, the state of California passed legislation requiring a mandatory prison sentence for burglary. As a result, the researchers were uncertain if the number of reported burglaries recorded during the project were affected by the new police procedures or due to the new law. Often, the only thing which researchers can do when an historical event occurs in the middle of their experiment is report that it occurred and let the findings be interpreted accordingly.

2. **Maturation** refers to the processes operating within research subjects as a function of the passage of time, including growing older, growing hungrier, or becoming more tired. Boredom could also be a problem which could affect the behavior of the research subjects.

3. **Testing** concerns the effect of taking a test upon the scores of a second testing. If the same instrument is used for the pre and post test, the subjects in the control group may be able to tease out what the instrument is designed to measure (i.e., fear of crime) and try to answer "the right way" rather than express their own true feelings.

4. **Instrumentation,** the concept of reliability was discussed in Chapter Four. If, upon repeated use, an instrument yields the

same results, it is considered to be reliable. But what would happen if your instrument was altered somehow between the pre and post tests? If there is some alteration in your instrument, the research results would be affected.

5. **Statistical Regression** is especially problematic when research subjects have been selected on the basis of their extreme scores or attributes. "Regression toward the Mean" is a statistical phenomenon which operates in nature. Any extreme attribute tends to be balanced out over time. The problem, therefore, is that extreme subjects tend to improve over time regardless of the treatment. For example, in his book, *The Future of Imprisonment*, Norval Morris[15] outlines a new prison model which he would like to test using the "toughest group of inmates." Morris proposes the use of a classical experimental design to assign such inmates to his model institution, but it is clear that statistical regression could be a particular threat to his proposed experiment. If these inmates are so "bad" to begin with, their behavior may simply regress toward the mean.

6. **Experimental Mortality** has to do with the loss of subjects from your experimental and control groups. If large numbers of subjects "drop out" for whatever reason, the groups may change so much that they are no longer comparable. Thus, the major strength of randomization is violated. Researchers conducting recidivism studies have particular problems with mortality since parolees are often mobile and do not leave forwarding addresses and they often literally die while on supervision.

7. **Selection Biases,** remember, the groups must be comparable to begin with. If techniques other than random assignment are used (to be discussed later), selection biases may affect the research results. Put simply, you do not wish to compare apples to oranges. Researchers should not put all the "best risks" in the experimental group and then compare them to a group of poor risks.

8. **Interactions of the Above Problems.** To make matters worse, it is possible that your research can be affected by combinations of the problems just mentioned. The design proposed by Morris could not only be subject to problems due to statistical regression, but also due to maturation. And what would happen to the research results if a riot or escape occurred during the study?

Other internal validity questions of special interest to criminal justice researchers have been identified by Adams:[1]

9. **Masking.** Experimental treatments may have opposite effects upon different kinds of subjects. Vito[17] has suggested that it is simply illogical to assume that all members of the experimental group were amenable to or served equally by a correctional treatment program. Unless some measure of the effectiveness of the treatment among the experimental subjects is included in the study, masking could cloud the findings by failing to make such differentiations in the experimental group.

10. **Contamination of Data.** If the subjects in the control group become exposed to the treatment, their post-program performance may be effected. This may have been one of the problems regarding the controversial Kansas City Preventive Patrol Experiment.[14] The treatment in this experiment was proactive police patrolling — a test of deterrence theory. The experimental neighborhoods received proactive patrolling, the reactive (control) areas underwent traditional patrolling (police responding to incoming calls for service and patrolling only the perimeter of the beat or an adjacent proactive beat), while officers in the control sections were to patrol as they normally would. The problem was that the 15 neighborhoods in the study were adjacent to one another. Was the treatment clearly isolated? In fact, Farrington[9] does not include the Kansas City experiment in his review of experimental programs because he felt that the selection of the beats and their small size defeated the experimental design structure.

11. **"Erosion" of the Treatment Effect.** The gradual or abrupt disappearance of performance superiority shown by the experimental group in the early months after treatment may decrease. This problem could be especially pronounced if the researcher is following the performance of the experimental subjects over a long period of time.

Finally, Cook and Campbell[6] have listed five additional threats to internal validity:

12. **Causal Time Order.** If somehow the time order between the treatment and the measure of the dependent variable (post-test) is fouled up, it is obvious that the causal relationship between variables is no longer being tested.

13. **Diffusion or Imitation of Treatment.** If the respondents in the control group can communicate with the members of the experimental group, they each may discover information intended for the other group. Put simply, the physical closeness of the two

groups may render them equal by exposing them both to the treatment. The Provo Experiment was plagued by this problem since both the experimental and control (probation) groups were supervised by the same probation office.

14. **Compensatory Equalization of Treatments.** When the experimental treatment provides goods or services generally believed to be desirable, the experimenter (or administrators in charge of a project) may be sympathetic toward the control group and provide them with some compensatory benefit, such as special attention. Of course, this special attention would thus become another form of treatment and the original design would suffer.

15. **Compensatory Rivalry by Respondents Receiving Less Desirable Treatments.** When the assignment of persons to experimental or control groups is made public (as is frequently required by ethical and legal considerations), competition may be generated. In particular, the control group (the natural underdog) may be motivated to perform at the highest possible level.

16. **Resentful Demoralization of Respondents Receiving Less Desirable Treatments.** This potential response is very much related to rivalry. The control group may become demoralized about the conditions of the research and thus perform more poorly than the experimental group or get angry and revolt.

These problems are not insurmountable. They have been presented because the researcher must be aware of them in order to combat them. Some can be dealt with through the use of randomization and the classical experimental design (i.e., selection bias and statistical regression). Others can be handled by careful monitoring of the conduct of the research. It is vital that the experimental and control groups are kept separate and that the integrity of the treatment is maintained. Exposure of the control group to the treatment must be avoided at all costs. It is clear that when the subjects in both groups are aware that an experiment is being conducted, the researcher must take some steps to see that compensation, rivalry, and demoralization do not occur.

THREATS TO EXTERNAL VALIDITY

The threats to external validity are concerned with the generalizability of the research findings. Generalizability simply means that the results of the study are applicable to other persons in other settings. The key question is: did something happen during the conduct of our experiment which makes it so unique that our findings have no meaning to the outside world? The answer to this question often resides in the manner in which the original population of subjects (or "pool of eligibles") was selected. Sampling techniques will be discussed in the next chapter which can help to solve some of the following problems.

Campbell and Stanley[5] identified four basic threats to external validity:

1. **The Reactive Effects of Testing.** The pre-test could increase or decrease the sensitivity (or awareness) of the respondents to the treatment so they are no longer like their counterparts in the outside world.

2. **The Inactive Effect of Selection Bias.** If your research group is not representative of the general population, your findings will not be generalizable. For example, a victimization study conducted in the most affluent section of a city would not yield results which would be representative of the entire city.

3. **The Reactive Effects of Experimental Arrangements.** This problem occurs when the subjects of the experiment become aware of their status. This phenomenon has been termed the **Hawthorne Effect** and it was experienced by researchers attempting to determine the effect of changes in working conditions on employee satisfaction and productivity. Research by Roethlisberger and Dickson (see Babbie[3]) in the "bank wiring room" of the Western Electric Works in Chicago revealed that the experimental group reacted favorably to any change in treatment which the experimenters instituted. In other words, the experimental subjects were responding to the attention given to them by the researchers, regardless of the treatment.

One way to combat the Hawthorne Effect is to utilize a **double blind experiment** in which neither the experimenters nor the research subjects know when the treatment is being administered. This technique is especially valuable in medical experiments. For example, Allen and his colleagues[2] tested the drug imipramine pamoate on an experimental group of incarcerated sociopaths to determine if the drug could alter their behavior. The drug was given to experimental and control group subjects in orange juice at the prison treatment center. No one on the project in the institution and none of the subjects knew whether the drug or the orange juice placebo was being administered. In this fashion, the researchers could determine if any differences in behavior were due to the drug, not due to any "coaching" by the experimenters. It was discovered that the sociopathic prisoners who received the drug felt and performed better than their counterparts in the control group.

4. **Multiple-Treatment Interference.** This can be a problem when more than one treatment is applied to the same respondents. Here, it would be difficult to separate the effects of the different treatments and the research results would be muddled.

One of the methods suggested by Campbell and Stanley[5] to combat problems of external validity is the **Solomon Four Group Design** (see Figure 6.3). This design is a combination of the classical experiment (Groups 1 and 2) and what is termed the **post-test only control group design** (Groups 3 and 4). To illustrate the functions of the Solomon four group design, let us use the following hypothetical example. We wish to assess the effectiveness of a counseling program which has been established to increase the sensitivity of police officers toward rape victims. Using random assignment, all officers in the department are assigned to one of the four groups. Groups 1 and 2 are enrolled in the program and thus are experimental groups, while groups 3 and 4 function as control groups. If the treatment is effective, we would expect that the officers in group 1 will be more sympathetic toward rape victims following the program (Comparison A). Group 1 officers should be more sympathetic than those in group 2 (Comparison B). Comparisons C and D should reveal a favorable treatment effect for group 3 officers in comparison to officers in groups 2 and 4. In this manner, the Solomon design helps to control any interaction between testing and the stimulus. It also provides a greater number of comparisons than the classical experiment.

Campbell and Stanley[5] also make a strong case for the post-test only control group design as a method to control for the effect of testing. Since the groups are assigned at random, they should be comparable so the pre-test may be a luxury which the researcher cannot afford.

The classical experiment, therefore, is not the only form of research design. It does, however, serve as the point of departure for other designs which attempt to approximate its key features.

THE QUASI-EXPERIMENTAL DESIGN

This design is the mirror image of the classical experiment with one key difference: the absence of random assignment. As previously men-

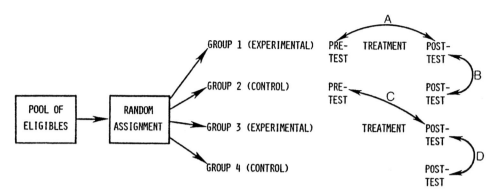

FIGURE 6-3: The Solomon Four Group Design

tioned, it is not always possible to implement the classical experiment. Yet, it is vital that a group is constructed to compare findings generated by the experimental group. Thus, a **comparison group** is selected using a method other than random assignment to insure that it is comparable to the experimental group.

Our example here is the evaluation of a prison-based treatment program for drug/alcohol abusing inmates (see Vito[17]). We need to find a group of inmates in the same prison who have the same problem, but who were **never involved in the program in any way.** After all, if we selected inmates who were excluded from the program, we would commit the error of selection bias. Similarly, if we chose inmates who dropped out of the program, the data would be contaminated because the comparison group would have been exposed to the treatment. What is left? Adams[1] suggests screening inmates who were considered for, but **for reasons of their own,** decided not to take part in the program — a **self-drop group.** Before such a group can be considered however, two important considerations must be checked out. First, the researcher must be certain that such inmates were not thrown out of the program by project administrators (Beware of selection bias!). Second, you must be certain that these inmates were never enrolled in or exposed to the treatment (contamination of data problem). It would also be possible to check for eligible inmates who were simply unaware of the program. It is also possible to use a variation of the matching technique (again the missing element is random assignment). Here, the experimenter would construct a comparison group which was identical to the experimental group on a number of known variables (i.e., age, race, prior record, present offense, education, marital status, etc.).

In any event, since randomization was not utilized, it is necessary to record relevant personal and socio-demographic information on such inmates and compare them directly to the experimental group. If differences do exist, it would be necessary to control for them statistically. Remember that the crucial issue here is that the experimental and comparison groups must be similar. The problem is that, even if you determine that the two groups are comparable, they may still differ on some important attribute which was beyond your means to measure. This is not a problem when random assignment is used, hence the power of the classical experimental design.

However, since it is not always possible to use random assignment, the quasi-experiment gives you another possibility to conduct accurate research. Quite simply, it may not be possible for you to do anything else and it is especially valuable when performing evaluation research (see Chapter Eleven).

NON-EXPERIMENTAL DESIGNS

Non-experimental designs take a variety of forms which emphasize description and which typically fail to make a comparison between the experimental group and another group of subjects. Typically, they are undertaken out of necessity because they, like the quasi-experimental design, offer a feasible alternative to research when the classical experiment is impossible to conduct. The chief problem is that the researcher is then unable to protect the integrity of the research results and clearly state that they reflect the effect of the treatment and not some other force.

The first type of non-experimental design is the **case study.** The case can be an individual (a professional criminal), an event (a police strike), or a place (Alcatraz). This type of design is capable of generating great quantities of descriptive information which can be used by policy makers. It is especially valuable in time of rapid change because it allows you to respond immediately to an historical event or a **natural experiment** — i.e., the effect of a judicial order on the operations of a prison[11] or a change in sentencing policy.[16]

The second type is the **time series design.** It is most often concerned with the analysis of trends over time to project future events. Typically, correlation and regression analysis (see Chapter 2) are used to make this determination. Data from previous years (or some other time frame) are used to make a prediction. It is used by prison administrators to plan for space needs in the future to analyze crime rates, or to anticipate the effect of a new law (i.e., mandatory prison sentence for drunk drivers).

The **cohort analysis** examines the behavior of a particular group over time. As defined by Adams,[1] cohorts are artificially constructed groups that share some common experience (i.e., involvement in the same program, graduating from the police academy in the same year). Their performance over time is then recorded. Probably the most famous cohort analysis was conducted by Wolfgang, Figlio, and Sellin[19] in which they tracked the delinquency record of a birth cohort of boys born in 1945 who lived in Philadelphia from their tenth to eighteenth birthdays. They discovered that 35 percent of the boys had some type of contact with the police and that about 50 percent of the juveniles who commit an offense are likely to commit another.

Probably the most common type of non-experimental design is the **before-after study.** This design is simply the first half of the experimental design. The performance of the experimental group is recorded before and after the treatment is administered. It is the simplest design but, due to the absence of comparison, it fails to document the effectiveness of the treatment. It is commonly used when it is difficult to construct a comparison or control group—i.e. to evaluate the effectiveness of a burglary prevention program in a particular neighborhood.[18]

CONCLUSION

This chapter reviewed the basic elements of research design—the blueprint for research. A number of key points were made. First of all, the researcher should attempt to use the soundest possible design. When random assignment cannot be conducted, several alternatives to the classical experiment do exist. The researcher must be aware of and plan to combat threats to internal and external validity to protect the accuracy of the research findings. Finally, it should be clear that sound research does not occur by accident. Careful planning of the conduct of the research is required.

KEY TERMS

Classical experiment
Matching

Non-experimental design
Provo Experiment
Quasi-experimental design
Random assignment
Threats to external validity
Threats to internal validity

STUDY GUIDE

1. What are the key features of the classical experiment? How was the Provo Experiment constructed?
2. Review the threats to internal and external validity.
3. How can a quasi-experiment be designed? Design one to evaluate the impact of a Citizens Crime Watch program.

REFERENCES

1. Adams, Stuart: *Evaluative Research in Corrections.* Washington, D.C.: U.S. Department of Justice, March, 1975.
2. Allen, Harry E., Dinitz, Simon, Foster, Thomas W., Goldman, Harold, and Lindner, Lewis A.: Sociopathy: An experiment in internal environmental control. *American Behavioral Scientist,* 20: 215-226, 1976.
3. Babbie, Earl: *The Practice of Social Research.* Belmont, CA: Wadsworth, 1983.
4. Baunach, Phyllis Jo: Random assignment in criminal justice research: Some ethical and legal issues. *Criminology,* 17: 435-444, 1980.
5. Campbell, Donald T. and Stanley, Julian C.: *Experimental and Quasi-Experimental Designs for Research.* Chicago: Rand McNally, 1963.
6. Cook, Thomas D. and Campbell, Donald T.: *Quasi-Experimentation: Design and Analysis Issues for Field Settings.* Boston: Houghton Mifflin, 1979.
7. Empey, LaMar T.: The provo experiment: Research and findings. In Radzinowicz, Leon and Wolfgang, Marvin E. (Eds.): *Crime and Justice, Volume III: The Criminal in Confinement.* New York: Basic Books, 1971, pp. 272-281.
8. Empey, LaMar T., and Rabow, Jerome: The provo experiment: Theory and design. In Radzinowicz, Leon and Wolfgang, Marvin E. (Eds.): *Crime and Justice, Volume III: The Criminal in Confinement.* New York: Basic Books, 1971, pp. 266-271.
9. Farrington, David P.: Randomized experiments in crime and justice. In Tonry, Michael and Morris, Norval (Eds.): *Crime and Justice: An Annual Review of Research.* Chicago: University of Chicago Press, 1983, pp. 257-308.
10. Finckenauer, James O.: *Scared Straight! and the Panacea Phenomenon.* Englewood Cliffs, NJ: Prentice-Hall, 1982.

11. Harris, M. Kay and Spillner, D.P.: *After Decision: Implementation of Justice Decrees in Correctional Settings.* Washington, D.C.: National Institute of Law Enforcement and Criminal Justice, 1977.

12. Hatry, Harry P., Winnie, Richard E., and Fisk, Donald M.: *Practical Program Evaluation for State and Local Government Officials.* Washington, D.C.: The Urban Institute, 1973.

13. Kerlinger, Fred N.: *Foundations of Behavioral Research.* New York: Holt, Rinehart and Winston, 1973.

14. Kelling, George L., Pate, Tony, Dieckman, Duane, and Brown, Charles E.: *The Kansas City Preventive Patrol Experiment: A Summary Report.* Washington, D.C.: Police Foundation, 1974.

15. Morris, Norval: *The Future of Imprisonment.* Chicago: The University of Chicago Press, 1974.

16. Travis III, Lawrence F.: The case study in criminal justice research: Applications to policy analysis. *Criminal Justice Review,* 8: 46-51, 1983.

17. Vito, Gennaro F.: Does it work? Problems in the evaluation of a correctional treatment program. *Journal of Offender Counseling, Services and Rehabilitation,* 7: 5-22, Fall, 1982.

18. Vito, Gennaro F., Longmire, Dennis R., and Kenney, John P.: Burglary suppression: A program analysis. *Journal of Contemporary Criminal Justice,* 2: 11-14, June, 1984.

19. Wolfgang, Marvin E., Figlio, Robert M., and Sellin, Thorsten: *Delinquency in a Birth Cohort.* Chicago: The University of Chicago Press, 1972.

20. Wood, Michael T.: Random assignment to treatment groups: A strategy for judicial research. *Criminology,* 17: 230-241, 1979.

CHAPTER SEVEN

PRINCIPLES OF SAMPLING

IN THIS CHAPTER, we are going to discuss the fundamentals of sampling. Whether or not you realize it, people are involved in sampling everyday. Probably the most common example is when you "sample" a cookie or some pie, you are tasting a piece of the whole. You assume that the rest of the cookies or pie tastes like the sample you tried. Similarly, when you ask someone their opinion, or when you make a statement about some group based on your knowledge of a member of that group you are in fact using the principles of sampling. The selection of a sample is one of the most important functions in the research process. Whether a researcher is surveying the entire population, or selecting individuals to observe or interview, the way in which the sample is chosen will help determine the usefulness of the study. In this chapter we will examine sampling; its definition, and some of the more common types of samples found in criminal justice research.

THE ORIGINS OF SAMPLING

Sampling in social science has its origins in political polling. Every election season we are inundated with polls and predictions about political candidates. Polling has become so sophisticated that major news networks have predicted the winners before some states have ended their voting. How accurate are polls? Pollsters have the opportunity to check the accuracy of their polls through election day results. Although polls have become increasingly accurate, errors are still possible. Perhaps the best known example of a sampling error was the *Literary Digest's* prediction that Alfred Landon would beat Franklin D. Roosevelt in the 1936 presidential election.[1] This after polling an incredible two million people.

The *Digest* had accurately predicted the 1920, 1924, 1928, and 1932 election results. So what went wrong? The answer lies in the sampling frame used by the *Digest*. A sampling frame is the actual list of sampling units from which the sample is selected or drawn. The *Digest* selected names from the telephone directories and automobile registrations. Remember, the country was in the midst of the great depression in 1936, and only the more affluent had phones and cars. As a result, their sample contained a disproportionate number of Republicans and well-to-do individuals, and excluded the poor, who predominately voted for FDR.

The above example represents a common pitfall of sampling, a non-representative sample. A sample is non-representative if the population from which it is drawn does not closely approximate the aggregate characteristics of the population. In other words, if you select a piece of pie from an edge that got burned you might make an error in deciding that the entire pie was ruined.

Another well known example of polling error was the 1948 presidential election in which Thomas E. Dewey was picked as the winner by virtually every pollster. Perhaps the most famous pollster, George Gallup (who had correctly picked FDR in 1936), also erred in predicting Dewey. Gallup used a technique called quota sampling, in which the sample is chosen on the basis of one's knowledge of the population under consideration. For example, the proportion of males selected is the same as the proportion of males in the population. So if 45 percent of the population is male, 45 percent of the sample will be male, and so forth. Usually the quota percentages are provided from the census that are taken every ten years by the Federal government. For the 1948 election, a number of errors were made. First, the pollsters stopped polling in early October. Second, there were a large number of undecided voters. Finally, the quota upon which Gallup had relied was based on the 1940 census. World War II had resulted in major shifts in the character of the American population, particularly with regard to the urban migration that had occurred after the war.

While political polling is probably the most common form of sampling, the criminal justice researcher has made considerable use of this technique. Public attitudes about crime, punishment, the death penalty, and numerous other criminal justice topics abound. The *Sourcebook of Criminal Justice Statistics*,[14] lists over 114 different topics that address public attitudes toward crime. These range from questions concerning the media's coverage of crime stories, to ratings of police honesty and ethics. Sampling is not only commonplace, but necessary to study virtually all aspects of social phenomenon, including crime and criminal behavior. Consider for a moment that there are over 500,000 prisoners in America today.[12] Imagine if you wanted to measure their prior criminal record or their attitudes toward punishment. Not only would it be tremendously expensive to collect data on all of them, but it would take a considerable amount of time, and it actually could be less accurate than if we drew a sample. A data collection effort of that magnitude would require extensive record-keeping and a large number of staff. The chances of errors and inconsistency would increase because of the numbers and time involved. We could obtain the needed information, probably more accurately, and certainly faster and cheaper through sampling. This is exactly what the Bureau of Justice Statistics did when they wanted to examine the recidivism of prisoners.[7] They conducted interviews with a sample of 9,040 prisoners in 1974 and 11,397 in 1979 to collect information on prior convictions and incarcerations. They probably would have found the same results had they interviewed all prisoners, but it would have been much more difficult and expensive. Remember, the average election poll is based on a sample of approximately 2,000 out of millions of eligible voters, and most are amazingly accurate.

It should also be mentioned that sample elements are not always about people. Sample elements can include families, gangs, and organizations. For example, Clinard and Yeager examined corporate crime by selecting a sample of American corporations.[4] Similarly, probation departments, halfway houses, and even prisons can be the major element of a sample.

SAMPLING ERROR

Generally, the criminal justice researcher conducts his/her analysis on the basis of limited information. Due to the constraints of time and money, it is generally impossible, and certainly not necessary, to collect data from an entire population, so a sample is constructed. Thus, sampling involves the selection of a proportion of the population, or a sample, in an attempt to draw a conclusion about the population on the basis of the analysis of that sample. No matter how the sample is selected, there are two possible sources of error:

1. Probability or chance error.
2. Systematic bias — selecting the sample from only one point of the population.

Probability or chance error is exactly that. Despite following all the prescribed steps and precautions, it is possible to select a non-representative sample. Systematic bias occurs when the research consciously, or unconsciously selects a sample from only one part of the population. For example, if you wanted to study probationer recidivism rates and developed your sampling list from two counties in California; your sample might accurately reflect probationers in those counties, but it would not represent all probationers in California, let alone the entire country. This is exactly what the Rand Corporation did in their study of felony probationers.[11] They selected a sample of 1,672 individuals who received probation in Los Angeles and Alamenda counties in California, and examined their recidivism rates. They found a rearrest rate of 65 percent over a 40 month period and concluded that, "felony probation does pose a serious threat to public safety." Well, maybe it does in those two counties in California, but similar studies conducted in Kentucky[16] and Missouri[8] found recidivism rates of only 22 percent over a similar time period. Unfortunately, the Rand study received wide distribution and attention, when in fact their conclusions were not justified or necessarily valid outside of the two counties they sampled.

Another example of systematic bias is the new form of telephone polling in which television viewers call in their "votes" on a 900 prefix (usually there is a 50 cent charge). As one television executive noted, "it looks like a poll, it sounds like a poll, but it isn't a poll."[2] Indeed, even though the results are often presented as scientific, they are not. The results of such tallies are skewed because the people who respond are not randomly selected. The phones used all handle the same number of calls a minute, which gives callers from a sparsely populated area a better chance to get through than those callers from a densely populated area.

As we see from the above examples, the real danger in biased samples is evident when the results are presented as representative of a population. When this occurs, the public is misled, and officials that make policy decisions can be seriously misinformed, resulting in bad policy.

TYPES OF SAMPLES

Basically, there are two types of samples:

1. Probability: where every member of the population is given an equal chance for selection.

2. Non-probability: where every member of the population is not given an equal chance of being selected.

Probability Samples

There are a number of different types of probability samples that can be employed by the researcher. We shall examine some of the more common types of probability samples used by criminal justice researchers.

Sample Random Samples

With simple random sampling each population member is assigned a unique number and sample members are selected through the use of a table of random numbers. Each member of the population is theoretically given a equal chance of being selected. Simple random sampling is the basis of experimental research where the experimental and control groups are assigned randomly. One example of simple random sampling would be state lotteries in which numbered balls are selected at random. Each ball or number has an equal chance of being selected.

The major advantage of random sampling is that it allows for the use of statistical probabilities which are required in many statistical tests (see Chapter Two). Even though you are not always assured of true representativeness, (remember there is always chance error) simple random sampling is the basis of most statistical techniques.

The problem with the simple random sampling is that it is not always possible to develop a complete list of the population. Indeed, the larger the population, the more difficult this task becomes. If for example, one wished to draw a random sample of probationers from the entire population of probationers it would be very difficult, if not virtually impossible, to generate an accurate list of the entire population. In many instances it is impossible to put together a complete list of the population. Therefore, the findings can be assumed to only be representative of some of the elements that make up the sampling frame.

One technique that has been widely used by pollsters is the random digit dialing technique, in which telephone numbers are randomly dialed. Due to the fact that over 95 percent of the population in the United States have a telephone, this technique is highly reliable and is considered a form of simple random sampling.[15] Obviously, not everyone has a phone, particularly the very poor or homeless, or the institutionalized (such as prisoners), but as a technqiue for measuring the general public's attitudes or opinions, this sampling procedure is very accurate.

Stratified Random Sampling

With stratified random sampling the population is divided into strata, (i.e., blacks, whites, Chicanos in prison), and a random sample is selected within each strata proportionate to the size of that segment of the population. Stratified random samples do not require a complete list of all the members of the population, but rather some knowledge of the proportions of the population according to some characteristic. The most common characteristics used for selection are demographic factors such as race, sex, age, or factors related to the nature of the study such as criminal record. The major advantage of stratified sampling is that it is a method for obtaining a greater degree of representativeness, thus decreasing the probability of sampling error. Remember, all samples have as a source of error random, or probability error. By producing more homogeneous subsets of the population you reduce the error in the variables selected for stratification to near zero. In other words, with a simple random sample you have the chance of selecting a disproportionate number of males, or whites, or personal offenders and so forth. With stratified sampling you would eliminate this error for those variables selected for stratification.

Cluster Sampling

The use of cluster sampling involves dividing the population into clusters such as census tracts, sections, blocks, neighborhoods, and the like, and then selecting a random sample within each cluster. Cluster sampling can be very useful when it is impossible to develop a complete listing of the population under study. However, as is often the case, the population elements may already be grouped into subpopulations, and a list of those groups may exist. For example, if you wanted to survey all inmates held in prison you probably could not establish a list of the entire population, but you could identify all the prisons in the country. Next, you could take a sample of prisons and obtain a list of inmates for the identified prisons. Each of the lists would then be sampled to provide the sample of inmates. This technique is particularly useful when interviews are being conducted since it greatly reduces time and costs, however, it does yield a less accurate sample.

Other forms of sampling include multistage sampling which involves the combination of stratified or cluster sampling or even other forms of sampling. For example, in selecting your sample of prisons you might initially stratify your list of prisons by type of institution, i.e., maximum, medium, minimum, closed security, geographic region, or size.

Once you have grouped the primary sampling units you can select cases according to simple random, stratified, or even cluster sampling methods.

Non-Probability Sampling

There are situations when it is impossible or undesirable to use random sampling techniques. When this occurs, the researcher must choose between a non-probability sample or scrapping the study altogether. In the field of criminal justice, random samples are oftentimes difficult to obtain due to the state of criminal justice information and data, costs, and human subject research restrictions. There are also situations where a list simply cannot be developed. If, for example, you wanted to study juvenile gangs it is impossible to obtain, or even to create a list of juvenile gang members. You would be forced to use a non-probability sample. Of course, this is better than no sample at all. Several of the more common types of non-probability samples include the availability, judgment, accidental, and quota samples.

Availability Sample

This technique involves selecting a group that is available for study. This is particularly relevant when the researcher is faced with the decision to either go with what is available or abandon the study. For example, delinquency studies are often conducted from readily available (incarcerated) delinquents. Many researchers would not scrap a study because of their inability to acquire or construct a random sample, but given the limitations of the sample it is important to remember that the generalization of the results are usually limited to the group under study.

Judgment Sample

Also known as a purposive sample, judgment samples involve taking a group which, based on the researchers' knowledge of the population, seems to be representative of all members. Judgment samples can be particularly useful if you are studying a group that is fragmented and difficult to identify. For example, if you were interested in studying motorcycle gang members you might have to settle for a certain group or gang, who, in your judgment represented a good cross-section of motorcycle gang members.

Judgment samples are fairly common in field research, where the research chooses subjects because they seem to represent the population under study. If you wanted to study the Ku Klux Klan it is highly doubt-ful that you could establish a sampling frame. Instead, you might focus your efforts on one state chapter and attempt to study that group.

Quota Sampling

Quota sampling involves a form of non-probability stratified sam-pling in which cases are selected according to a characteristic propor-tionate to the population under study. If, for example, your target population was a sample of prisoners in a particular state, you would need to determine the proportions that were male and female, black, white, or chicano, and so forth. There is no random selection involved. Once you established your quotas for each category, you would then se-lect adequate numbers to fill the quotas. Another problem is that the quota frame (i.e., proportions of each subgroup) may not be accurate, resulting in a biased sample similiar to the Gallup poll during the 1948 presidential election.

Accidental Sample

With an accidental sample the researcher takes whoever comes along. We see this technique used by newspaper and television reporters, the so called "person on the street" technique. Obviously, this results in a very unscientific and biased sample.

Snowball Sample

Snowmen usually start with a snowball that is rolled until it becomes large enough to form the body of a snowman. Snowball sampling de-rives its name from the process. Let's say that you are interested in studying professional thieves, and you find a suitable candidate. After you have interviewed this person you would ask for the name or an in-troduction to another professional thief, and so on until you had a suit-able sample. Snowball samples are best used when you are trying to study a hard to reach group.[9] For example, in his study of prostitution, Bryan obtained a sample of "call girls" by using a snowball sampling technique.[3] Most of the call girls studied were provided through other prostitutes. Lockwood also used this technique in selecting a sample of inmates that had been the target of sexual aggression in prison.[10] Prison staff charged with handling inmate crises referred to 34 targets of ag-gressors for study. Both of these examples represent "hard to reach" groups that are not readily available for study. By using a snowball sam-pling procedure, Bryan and Lockwood were able to gather valuable information about two relatively unknown areas of deviant behavior.

It is important to remember that the usefulness of a sample is directly related to the ability of the sample to provide information and a description of the population from which it was drawn. Probability samples are designed to eliminate or reduce bias, however, there may be situations in which non-probability samples are justified or necessary.

Sampling in Criminal Justice: Some Examples

We will now turn our attention to several examples of sampling techniques in criminal justice settings. Each of these studies involved the identification of a sample of respondents in order to address different research questions. In the next chapter we shall examine how these were used in survey research, but for now we shall just concentrate on the ways in which the samples were identified and selected.

Criminal Victimization in the United States

Beginning in 1972, the Law Enforcement Assistance Administration and the Bureau of the Census began a national victimization study based on a stratified multistage cluster sample[5] survey, part of the National Crime Survey (see Chapter 4), which involved a very expensive and complicated sampling procedure that used as its basis for the sampling frame housing units of virtually all types. The sampling units for the first stage of the sample were counties, groups of counties or large metropolitan areas. These units were divided into strata by grouping the primary sampling units with similar demographic characteristics as determined by the census. From each stratum, one area was selected for the sample. The remaining stages of sampling were designed to ensure a self-weighting probability sample of housing units within each of the selected areas. This was followed by the selection of clusters of approximately four housing units each from within each enumeration district. A total of approximately 69,000 housing units were designated for the sample. For the field interviews, the sample was divided into six groups, each of which contained housing units whose occupants were to be interviewed every six months over a three year period. A total of 57,000 of the 69,000 households were subsequently surveyed. All told, 96 percent of the eligible households, or some 123,000 persons, participated in the survey.

Even as elaborate as this sample was it excluded Armed Forces personnel living in military barracks and institutionalized persons, such as prisoners. Naturally, it would also exclude the homeless, since by defini-tion they do not have a housing unit.

Police Innovation

In a recent study by Skolnick and Bayley of police strategy and inno-vation in six American cities, the authors describe their technique for se-lecting the sample:[13]

> Our plan was to undertake mini-ethnographic studies of six cities: Denver, Detroit, Houston, Neward, Oakland, and Santa Ana. This was not a scientific sample. The cities were selected because they were scattered fairly well throughout the country (the Southeast being the obvious exception); some were already known for innovation; some were recognized as being particularly difficult to police; some we had worked in already; and in all we had assured access.

Here we see an example of a judgment sample, since in the opinion of the researchers these six cities met their needs. It was also somewhat of an availability sample since they used access as one of their selection criteria. In other words, these six cities were, in judgment of the re-searchers, good cases for study, and they were available, since they had access. This type of sampling procedure is not uncommon in a study of this kind, where essentially six case studies are being conducted to de-velop some in-depth information about a relatively unknown subject.

Attitudes Toward Crime

In their study of attitudes toward juvenile rehabilitation in Illinois, Cullen et al., used a non-probability sample that was part judgment and part availability. They describe their sampling technique as follows:[6]

> . . . questionnaires were mailed or distributed to a sample of 1,146 people. Of this number, 200 were residents of Springfield, the capital of Illinois. The residents' names were drawn indiscriminately from the city's telephone directory; however, no random numbers table was em-ployed. This directory was also used to obtain a sample of 200 lawyers (approximately 450 are listed). Two hundred circuit judges were se-lected from a state-wide roster. A sample of 40 correctional adminis-trators was arrived at by sending surveys to the warden and one additional top administrative official at 20 correctional institutions throughout the state. Further, all 236 members of the legislature (56 senators, 177 representatives) were surveyed. Seventy guards and 200 inmates sampled were located at Sheridan Correctional Center, a minimum-medium security prison of approximately 400 inmates. Questionnaires were distributed to all guards present at the roll call of

two of the institution's three shifts, while inmates were provided with and returned surveys through institutional mail. To minimize potential nonresponse problems, only inmates with the equivalent of an eighth-grade education or above received the survey.

Although this was not a probability sample, it did permit the researchers to gauge the views of Illinois officials. While it certainly lacks generalizability, it provides a basis for future research, and a rough indicator of attitude toward juvenile rehabilitation in Illinois.

Corporate Crime

An example of a non-probability sample that involved organizations rather than individuals can be seen in Clinard and Yeager's study of corporate crime.[4]

In 1980, Clinard and Yeager published the results of their study of corporate crime. Based on a sample of 582 corporations, they developed their sampling frame by systematically analyzing federal administrative, civil, or criminal actions initiated or completed by 25 federal agencies. Thus, they focused their study on corporations that had actions initiated (similar to an arrest) and actions completed (conviction) by one of the 25 federal agencies. As a result, they tapped "only the tip of the iceberg of total violations." Of course it would be nearly impossible to include all types of violations against these corporations or their subsidiaries, and again, it could be argued that this type of sample is certainly better than abandoning the study altogether.

Guns and Crime

In their study of felons and their firearms, Wright and Rossi illustrate the compromises that are often involved in sampling an incarcerated population.[17] The purpose of their research was to survey incarcerated felons in state prisons about how and why they purchased, carried, and used guns. A cluster sampling technique was chosen since prisoners are located in clusters (prisons). First they chose states, then prisons within states, and finally, prisoners within prisons. They originally wanted to select states based on the density of private gun ownership, and the stringency of state firearms regulation. They also wanted a reasonable geographical spread. One problem was the willingness of states to participate, and as a result they only approached states where they had reason to believe they would cooperate. Once the states were identified they hoped to survey inmates at maximum-security institutions, but in most cases they were not permitted to do so. In fact, in nearly every instance, the decision as to which prison they would be allowed to study was made by the correctional officials. In the prisons themselves, new restrictions were imposed on which men they could interview. Inmates in protective custody, in disciplinary confinement, in psychiatric wards, or on death row were excluded. The researchers also decided against including certain offenders in the sampling frame. These included misdemeanants, women, and offenders that had been incarcerated prior to January 1979. Once the sampling frame was completed, they either surveyed all inmates in the institution (if the eligible population was less than 400), or they drew a simple random sample from the prison census list.

The Wright and Rossi study is a good example of where a combination of sampling techniques were used, and where constraint imposed by the environment led to compromise and modification. Despite the departure from their original sampling plan, their research represents a major study of weapon behavior on the part of convicted felons.

CONCLUSION

This chapter has reviewed the basics of sampling and how it can be applied to criminal justice research. As we have seen, sampling can take many forms, ranging from random sampling techniques where every member of the population is given an equal chance of being selected, to non-probability samples such as the availability sample where the research selects whoever is available or accessible.

Despite the constraints and problems of sampling within the criminal justice field, many important and groundbreaking research has been conducted using less than ideal sampling procedures. Ultimately, the research findings should only be generalized to the sampling frame from which the sample was selected.

KEY TERMS

Population
Sampling Frame
Sampling Element
Polling
Systematic Bias
Chance Error

Cluster Sample
Stratified Sample
Availability Sample
Quota Sample

STUDY GUIDE

1. What is sampling, and why is it so important?
2. Are pollsters always accurate? What are some of the common pitfalls of polling?
3. Describe the two types of sampling error.
4. What is a probability sample? A non-probability sample?
5. What is the greatest problem with simple random sampling?
6. Describe a judgment sample. A snowball sample.
7. What are the types of situations in which a non-probability sample would be appropriate?
8. What were some of the constraints imposed on Wright and Rossi's study of firearms and inmates?

REFERENCES

1. Babbie, Earl: *Survey Research Methods.* Belmont, Wadsworth, 1973.
2. Belkin, Lisa: TV phone polls provoke controversy. *Cincinnati Enquirer.* Wednesday, July 8, 1987, pg. E-8.
3. Bryan, James H.: Apprenticeships in prostitution. *Social Problems.* 12: 287-297, 1965.
4. Clinard, Marshall, B., and Yeager, Peter C.: *Corporate Crime.* New York, Free Press, 1980.
5. Criminal Victimization in the United States, 1980: Washington, D.C., U.S. Department of Justice, Bureau of Justice Statistics, 1982.
6. Cullen, Francis T., Golden, Kathryn M., and Cullen, John B.: Is child saving dead? Attitudes toward juvenile rehabilitation in Illinois. *Journal of Criminal Justice, 11:* 1-13, 1983.
7. Examining Recidivism: Washington, D.C., U.S. Department of Justice, Bureau of Justice Statistics, February 1985.
8. Fichter, M., Hirschburg, P., and McGaha, J.: Felony probation: a comparative analysis of public risk to two states. Paper presented at the annual meeting of the American Society of Criminology, Atlanta, 1986.
9. Goodman, Leo, A.: Snowball sampling. *Annal of Mathematical Statistics, 32:* 148-170, March 1969.
10. Lockwood, Daniel: *Prison Sexual Violence.* New York, Elsevier, 1980.

11. Petersilia, Joan: Probation and felony offenders. *Federal Probation,* 49: 2-9, 1985.
12. Prisoners in 1985: Washington, D.C., U.S. Department of Justice, Bureau of Justice Statistics, June 1986.
13. Skolnick, Jerome H. and Bayley, David H.: *The New Blue Line, Police Innovation in Six American Cities.* New York, Free Press, 1986, pg. 6.
14. Soucebook of Criminal Justice Statistics—1985: Washington, D.C., U.S. Department of Justice, Bureau of Justice Statistics, 1986.
15. Tuchfarber, Alfred J., Klecka, William R., Bardes, Barbara A., and Oldendick, Robert W.: Reducing the cost of victim surveys. In Skogan, Wesley G. (Ed.): *Sample Surveys of the Victims of Crime.* Cambridge, Ballinger, 1976, pp. 207-221.
16. Vito, Gennaro F.: Felony probation and recidivism: replication and response. *Federal Probation, 50:* 17-25, 1986.
17. Wright, James D., and Rossi, Peter H.: *Armed and Considered Dangerous: A Survey of Felons and Their Firearms.* New York: Aldine De Gruyter, 1975.

CHAPTER EIGHT

SURVEY RESEARCH

OFTEN, THE researcher selects a sample in order to conduct a survey of some type. This survey can take on many forms, ranging from a mailed questionnaire to a personal interview. In today's world of marketing research and public opinion polls, virtually all of us have completed a survey of some type. Indeed, the expansion of consumer and marketing research has made surveys a very popular and widely used way of gathering information. This chapter will examine some of the forms that surveys can assume, and the ways in which they are applied to criminal justice research.

INTRODUCTION TO SURVEY RESEARCH

Survey research is generally conducted in order to make descriptive assertions about a population. It is not designed to determine **why** something exists, but rather, **what** the distribution looks like. Thus, survey research is the best method to collect original data for the purpose of describing a population too large to observe directly.

Survey research can, and often does involve large samples. This is a major advantage of surveys. This is made possible through mail or telephone surveys. Surveys can resemble a "snapshot" of the population, or be longitudinal in nature. A "snapshot" is where the researcher takes a picture of the population. For example, in the Cullen et al.,[3] study discussed in Chapter Seven, the sample in Illinois was asked about juvenile rehabilitation. This survey gave us a one time picture of how this sample of Illinois residents felt about this subject.

One form of survey is the longitudinal survey. A longitudinal survey is used when the researcher wishes to measure a population over time to determine how it changes. An example of a longitudinal survey would be the National Victimization Survey, where yearly measures are taken to determine crime rates from year to year. Other examples of longitudinal surveys would include public opinion polls about crime or other topics that are taken on a regular basis.

It is important to mention that regardless of the nature of the survey or the manner in which it is administered, it is always important to conduct a thorough review of the literature. This helps the researcher develop a conceptual framework for the study, and prevents "reinventing the wheel." There is nothing wrong with replicating a previous study, but the researcher should be aware of the major findings about a topic before he or she begins to work. Reviews of the literature also provide valuable information about the strengths or weaknesses of a particular method or technique. This may help prevent making the same mistakes.

Another tool used to design surveys is the pilot study. Generally, a pilot study involves testing the survey on a smaller scale. For example, in her study of prison classification, Van Voorhis conducted a pilot study using inmates at a Federal prison.[11] This pilot study was done in order to determine the advisability of a larger study. Extensive interviews were conducted with 56 inmates, and a number of predictors were found. Based on this pilot study, a much larger, federally funded effort is under way in which a minimum of 300 inmates will be interviewed and studied.

Surveys are not without their shortcomings. Some of the more prevalent weaknesses of survey research include the following:[1]

1. Standardization can be a problem. This is especially true when superficial questions are used in an attempt to deal with complex issues.
2. Survey research cannot deal with the context of social life. There will be no feel for the thinking or logic involved, nor the social context.
3. Direct observations can modify as field conditions warrant, but survey designs stay unchanged.
4. Artificiality tends to be a problem, and the respondent may not have thought about a question until they were asked.
5. Surveys cannot measure social action, they only collect self-reports or recollections of the past.

Surveys also tend to be weak on validity and strong on reliability. An awareness of these problems can help to partially offset them. In addition, surveys can be used in conjunction with other techniques that can compensate for these shortcomings.

PRINCIPLE TYPES OF SURVEYS

There are a number of ways in which surveys are administered. We will discuss some of the more common types of surveys used in criminal justice research.

Self-Administered Questionnaire

The self-administered questionnaire generally takes two forms, those that are handed-out to a group of respondents, and those that are mailed. A survey that is administered to a group of respondents gathered in one place is common when you have a captive audience, such as a prison population. In the Vito et al.,[10] study of an institutional drug/alcohol program, questionnaires were administered to inmates who "volunteered" with the inducement of a pack of cigarettes. Similarly, Wright and Rossi's study of firearms involved interviewing inmates within the institution. They agreed to pay overtime to the correctional officers that supervised the inmates, and contribute $100 to the prison library.[11] We also see this form of the self-administered survey used in market research. How many of us have been asked to fill out a questionnaire in a supermarket or in the parking lot of a shopping center?

Mail Survey

Mail surveys are the most typical self-administered form of data collection. Generally, they involve a questionnaire along with a letter of explanation and a return envelope mailed to the respondent. The mail questionnaire's popularity stems in part because it can be administered quickly and for relatively low cost. It also affords the researchers a wide range of coverage. After all, it costs the same to mail a letter to Alaska as it does to mail it across town.

Advantages

In addition to their low cost and timeliness, respondents may be more willing to reveal personal information with a mail questionnaire than they would be in a face-to-face interview. The nature of the mail survey may help the respondent feel more at ease in answering sensitive questions since privacy is virtually assured.

Another major advantage of the mail survey is that it affords a wide geographic range of coverage. A national survey will cost about the same as a local one, and it may also be more representative. Mail surveys also eliminate interviewer bias, since there are no interviewers involved.

Mail questionnaires are also more suitable in situations in which the respondent has to check or gather information. They also provide greater uniformity in the manner in which the questions are posed, and they afford a simple means of continued reporting over time, i.e., longitudinal surveys.

Disadvantages

Despite their low cost and wide range of coverage, mail questionnaires have some inherent problems. Perhaps the most prevalent problem is the response rate. Generally those that fail to respond fall into one of two categories: those that have not yet responded and those that refuse to respond. If a subject refuses to cooperate, the researcher should honor the request. Since this is usually a small percentage, oversampling can compensate for this problem. The more common non-response falls into the "have not yet responded" group. A number of strategies have been employed to increase response rates for mail surveys including follow-up letters, offering copies of results, appeals to altruism, endorsements from well-known individuals or organizations, renumeration, short instruments, certified mailings, and telephone follow-ups. Mail surveys have become so common that even the follow-up mailing response rates can be estimated.

One question that is often asked is "what is a sufficient response rate?" Unfortunately, there is no correct answer. Response rates will vary greatly from survey to survey depending on a number of factors including the type of sample surveyed, the follow-up method, length and complexity of the instrument, and so forth. Generally, a 40 percent response rate is considered very good, 60 percent excellent, and over that, you are doing exceptionally well. For example, the Cullen et al.,[3] survey resulted in a 37 percent response rate for the general public, 27.5 percent for the Illinois legislature, 43 percent for the inmates, and 44 percent for correctional officers. Overall, their response rate was 37 percent.

In another example, Cullen, Latessa, and Bryne[4] conducted a survey of Division I-A head football coaches concerning their attitudes about drug abuse and related issues in college football, which resulted in over a 62 percent response rate. In this survey the questionnaire included an endorsement from the athletic director of the researchers' university, and a promise to share with the coaches the results of the study. In addition, a variation of the Dillman[5] method of follow-up was utilized in which a letter was sent one week after the original questionnaire was mailed thanking them if they had responded and urging those that had not, to do so. Three weeks later another follow-up letter was sent along with a new copy of the survey. This technique is an effective way to increase the response rate, however, it does increase the costs, since another mailing must be conducted.

The problem with a low response rate is that there is no way of knowing whether or not those that did not respond differ from those that did. Related to this problem is the issue of bias. Mail surveys generally miss a certain segment of the population such as those without mailing addresses, i.e., the homeless, and the lower educated and illiterate. The result may be a homogeneous sample. Therefore, the real issue is not the response rate, but the randomness of the sample.

Mail questionnaires, as with surveys in general, also have the problems of artificiality, standardization, oversimplification, validity, and the inability to measure social actions. There is also the possibility that the respondent will misinterpret or misunderstand the question.

Face-to-Face Interviews

Although interviews can take on many different forms, the most common are, (1) the completely structured interview, in which respondents do little more than answer check-off questions, and (2) unstructured interviews in which open-ended questions are the rule rather than the exception. Obviously, these two types are not necessarily mutually exclusive. Many interviews include both formats.

Advantages

Unlike a questionnaire, an interview can almost eradicate the response rate problem. Ninety percent response rates and higher are not uncommon with an interview survey. Perhaps the greatest advantage of the interview is that more in-depth, detailed responses may be obtained. The interview can clear up any confusing questions, and there is less likelihood of missing information and "don't knows." The interviewer can also gather additional information simply through observation, i.e., gender, race, type of neighborhood, etc. Interviewers can also read questions to low educated respondents, and they are not restricted to mailing addresses; that is, they can go out into the field, thus gathering information from hard-to-reach populations. For example, Costin[2] interviewed "bag ladies" in New York City by going to the parks and areas where they frequented. Obviously, a mail or telephone survey would have been impossible with this sample. Likewise the Petersilia, Greenwood, and Lavin survey of career criminals discussed in Chapter Four involved the self-report method as a way to uncover crime.[8] It is doubtful if another form of survey would have been as fruitful as these structured interviews.

Face-to-face interviews also have the advantage of allowing the interviewer the gauge the tone of the respondent, and they can be more effective with complicated topics. You also have the advantage of knowing exactly who is responding to the survey. In addition, probes can be used to solicit additional information, or to clarify questions.

Disadvantages

While face-to-face interviews can yield more detailed information, there are a number of problems including: (1) Cost. Interviews can be extremely expensive, especially ones involving large samples spread over a wide area. (2) Interviewer effect. The interviewer must be very careful not to bias the responses by giving cues. If this occurs, the respondent may answer according to what he or she "believes" the interviewers want. Mistakes by interviewers in asking questions or recording information is also a problem. Interviewers may also avoid certain individuals out of fear or apprehension. While verification is possible, it is expensive. (3) Individual responses. This can be a problem with open-ended questions. The answers are such that they provide such a diverse range of responses as to make any type of aggregation meaningless.

Tips for Interviews

The following tips have been adapted from Babbie,[1] who has developed a list of tips or general rules for interviewing that can help reduce some of the problems and improve the quality of the responses:

1. Appearance and dress. Generally, the interviewer should be neat, clean, and if possible should dress similar to those being interviewed.

2. Familiarity with questions. The interviewer should follow the wording exactly and record the answers completely and accurately. Needless to say, the interviewers should understand the format and purpose of the survey. Training is very important.

3. Coordination and control. If more than one interviewer is being used, then careful control and supervision needs to be maintained. Again, training is very important.

4. Recording the interview. Responses can be recorded in several ways. Structured interviews are more amenable to written recording since most answers are simply checked off. More indepth interviews may require the use of a tape recorder. Permission must be obtained from the respondent before any recording is made. If recording is not possible, then the interviewers must be careful to record as closely as possible the answers, writing verbatim key points. Transcribing of written material should occur as soon as possible after the interview while the information is still fresh.

Telephone Interviews

Using the telephone to gather information has become very popular. Telephone interviews combine the low cost and wide range of the mail survey, with the relatively high response rate and personal contact of the face-to-face interview. While telephone surveys are limited to those with phones, nearly 97 percent of all households have phones.[9] Even unlisted numbers can be overcome by using a random digit dialing technique. As with other types of surveys, a variety of sampling techniques can be used with telephone surveys. The problem, of course, is **who** should be interviewed. Calling at different times can help assure a variety of family members, or quota sampling can be used. One unique technique that has been used to insure random selection is the "last birthday" method, in which the person in the household (above a certain age) with the last birthday is interviewed.[7]

Combining the mail survey and the telephone survey is another way to gather information. With this procedure, a questionnaire is mailed to the respondent and a telephone interview is used to gather the information. This technique is particularly useful when the unit of analysis is an organization and the information being requested might come from a variety of sources. For example, in a recent study of prison technology, Latessa et al.,[6] surveyed each state's department of corrections concerning the use of technology in prisons. A great deal of factual information was requested. Each state was mailed a questionnaire and asked to gather the information. A telephone follow-up was conducted and the information was relayed over the phone to an interviewer. In many cases the respondents simply completed the questionnaires and mailed them in, and in other cases virtually all the information was gathered over the phone. Follow-up for missing or incomplete information was easily done, and information was gathered from virtually all jurisdictions.

QUESTIONNAIRE CONSTRUCTION

Now that we have covered some of the ways in which surveys can be administered, we can turn our attention to the construction of the actual instruments used in collecting the information. The way in which a questionnaire is organized may effect the response rate, so it is important to follow some basic guidelines. First, begin with easy questions that are interesting, but nonthreatening. If your first question is "have you ever been sexually molested?" your survey will probably be over before it begins. Likewise, if you start with boring demographics, such as age, nationality, education, and so forth, you will likely turn off many of your respondents.

Another important consideration of questionnaire development is the order of the questions. The appearance of one question can affect the answers given to subsequent ones. For example, if you asked a number of questions about heinous or well-publicized crimes and then followed it with a question asking them to list and rank the most pressing problems facing the country, it is very likely that crime would be cited more and given a higher rating than it would have otherwise.

Structured Questions

Structured questions, also called closed-ended questions, provide a list of possible answers for the respondent. The problem is that the list of possible answers may overlook some relevant answers. You are essentially forcing the respondent to select one of the choices offered. One way to avoid this is to allow a space for "other." Closed-ended questionnaires are easier to complete, but the response categories should be exhaustive, and mutually exclusive. Closed-ended questions can include a large number of possible responses or ask for a "yes" or "no" response.

Unstructured Questions

Open-ended or unstructured questions allow the respondent to elaborate on the answers. These types of questions provide an opportunity for the respondent to give more detailed answers. Interviewers often use this technique to allow the respondent to answer at length about an issue or topic. Of course, one problem with open-ended questions is that they may result in irrelevant answers. This is particularly a problem with mail questionnaires, since there is no interviewer to clarify a question. When used with a mail survey, open-ended questions should be placed at the end of the instrument to insure that the closed-ended are answered. If they are placed first, the respondent may not complete the survey because it appears to be too complex. In many situations a combination of the two types of questions are used. Even if the questionnaire is predominately closed-ended, you may want to allow the respondent to provide additional information at the end of the survey with an open-ended question.

Guidelines for Questions

The following guidelines should be used when asking questions:[1]

1. Provide a clear introduction of the purpose of the survey.
2. Order the questions to establish a rapport with the respondent.
3. Write clear items.
4. Avoid double-barreled questions.
5. Respondents must be competent to answer the questions.
6. Questions should be relevant.
7. Short items are best.
8. Avoid negative items.
9. Avoid biased and slanted questions.
10. Cross-check questions.
11. Pre-test the instrument.
12. The questionnaire should look good.
13. Language should be pitted to the level of the respondent.
14. Use words with the same meaning to everyone, avoiding jargon.
15. Establish a frame of reference.
16. If examining unpleasant feelings, given an opportunity for a positive response.
17. Phrase questions so that they are not objectionable.
18. Go from general to specific.

Developing a questionnaire that meets all of these guidelines is essential if you wish to gather accurate, valid, and reliable information. The same points apply to most interview situations. Remember, if your questions are unclear, confusing, or misleading, the result will be responses that are unreliable.

THE IMPACT OF TECHNOLOGY IN PRISONS: AN EXAMPLE OF A SURVEY IN CRIMINAL JUSTICE

In the last chapter we presented several illustrations of sampling techniques that are found in criminal justice research. Each of these samples was done with a purpose, to **survey** the population. Let us now turn our attention to one example of a survey that includes several of the techniques discussed above.

Prison Technology

As we mentioned previously, Latessa and others[6] recently conducted a federally funded study designed to measure the impact of technology on prisons. In order to accomplish this task, they began by surveying all 52 jurisdictions in the United States that operate a prison system. This survey was administered using a combination mail/telephone technique. Surveys were mailed to all 52 jurisdictions, and questions were asked about their new prison construction, technology usage, management philosophy, and decision making criteria. A telephone follow-up was then conducted to determine who would be responsible for completing the instrument. Respondents were given the option of mailing in the questionnaire, or answering the questions over the phone. Many of the jurisdictions elected to mail in the instrument, however, missing or incomplete information was obtained over the telephone.

In addition to the "system" survey, 125 prisons built within the last ten years were also surveyed in a similar manner. This instrument was much more detailed, covering 34 pages, and asking questions related to security, communications, management information, and fire systems. Since this questionnaire was much more complex, usually more than one individual was required to gather the information. Telephone interviews took up to six hours to complete, and often had to be scheduled over a several day period.

Finally, six prisons were selected and visited by a team of researchers.

TABLE 8.1

PRISON TECHNOLOGY SURVEY

Is there a centralized management information system for your state/jurisdiction?

If so, how long has this system been in use?

Is this system located in the Department of Correction or in some other agency?

Which of the following functions are performed using this central management information system?

a.	inmate count	Yes ___	No ___
b.	inmate tracking	Yes ___	No ___
c.	intake/release	Yes ___	No ___
d.	payroll	Yes ___	No ___
e.	commissary accounts	Yes ___	No ___
f.	planning/evaluation	Yes ___	No ___
g.	medical	Yes ___	No ___
h.	other (please describe)	Yes ___	No ___

Overall, how satisfied or dissatisfied are you with the maintenance necessary for the perimeter security system?

1. VERY SATISFIED
2. SOMEWHAT SATISFIED
3. SOMEWHAT DISSATISFIED
4. VERY DISSATISFIED
0. INAPPROPRIATE

Had the installation of this system increased or decreased the number of staff required?

1. INCREASED
2. DECREASED
3. NO CHANGE
0. INAPPROPRIATE

Do you generally feel more safe or less safe with the security system?

1. MORE SAFE
2. LESS SAFE
3. ABOUT THE SAME

Correctional officers were asked to complete self-administered questionnaires concerning their attitudes about new technology. Structured interviews were then conducted with supervisory personnel and management staff. These interviews were designed to gather more in-depth information about the institution and its use of technology.

This study is unique since it included mail, telephone, self-administered and interview techniques. Table 8.1 illustrates some of the questions that were asked on these surveys, which included both closed- and open-ended questions.

CONCLUSION

Surveys are a common form of gathering information in the criminal justice setting. Surveys can take many forms, including mail and telephone surveys, self-administered questionnaires, and interviews. We have also seen that questionnaire development can be complex and difficult, and that each type of survey brings with it a particular set of strengths and weaknesses.

Surveys provide us with the ability to measure attitudes, factual information, and perceptions of a wide and virtually endless range of social phenomena, including crime.

KEY TERMS

Longitudinal Survey
Self-Administered Questionnaire
Telephone Interview
Dillman Method
Last Birthday Response
Structured Questions
Unstructured Questions

STUDY GUIDE

1. Why is survey research generally conducted?
2. What are the strengths of a survey? Weaknesses?
3. What are the advantages of a mail survey? Disadvantages?
4. What are the advantages of a face-to-face interview? Disadvantages?
5. What are some of the ways that a response rate can be increased with a mail survey.
6. Construct a ten-item questionnaire for self-administering. Include both closed- and open-ended questions.
7. What are some tips for interviewing?

REFERENCES

1. Babbie, Earl: *The Practice of Social Research,* Belmont, Wadsworth, 1986.
2. Costin, Charisse, T. "The Original Designer Label: Prototypes of New York City's Shopping-bag Ladies," Unpublished master's thesis, Rutgers University, 1981.

3. Cullen, Francis T., Golden, Kathryn M., and Cullen, John B.: Is child saving dead? Attitudes toward juvenile rehabilitation in Illinois. *Journal of Criminal Justice, 11:* 1-3, 1983.

4. Cullen, Francis, T., Latessa, Edward J., and Bryne, Joe: Lawlessness in collegiate athletics: A national survey of NCAA head football coaches. Paper presented at the annual meeting of the Academy of Criminal Justice Sciences, San Francisco, April 1988.

5. Dillman, Don A.: *Mail and Telephone Surveys: The Total Design Method.* New York, John Wiley and Sons, 1978.

6. Latessa, Edward J., Oldendick, Robert W., Travis, Lawrence F., and Noonan, Susan: *The Impact of Technology in Prisons,* draft report, Cincinnati, Institute of Policy Research, University of Cincinnati, 1988.

7. Oldendick, Robert W., Sorenson, Susan B., Tuchfarber, Alfred J., and Bishop, George F.: Last birthday respondent selection in telephone survey: a further test. Paper presented at the annual meeting of the Midwestern Association of Public Opinion Research, Chicago, 1985.

8. Petersilia, Joan, Greenwood, Peter W., and Lavin, Marvin: *Criminal Careers of Habitual Felons,* Santa Monica, Rand Corporation, 1977.

9. U.S. Bureau of the Census: 1979, *Statistical abstracts of the United States.* Washington, D.C.: U.S. Government Printing Office.

10. Vito, Gennaro F. and Kaitsa, George: 1977, *Marion Correctional Institution, drug/alcohol abuse therapeutic community: Project Papillon.* Columbus, Program for the Study of Crime and Delinquency, Ohio State University.

11. Van Voorhis, Patricia: 1988, A cross classification of five offender typologies: Issues of construct and predictive validity, *Criminal Justice and Behavior* (forthcoming).

12. Wright, James D. and Rossi, Peter H.: *Armed and Considered Dangerous: A Survey of Felons and Their Firearms.* New York, Aldine De Gruyter, 1975.

CHAPTER NINE

QUALITATIVE METHODOLOGY

CRIMINAL JUSTICE research, like all social research, attempts to answer one or more of three questions: "What are the characteristics of a given phenomenon?" "What caused it?" and "What are the consequences of it?" Attempts to answer the first questions are called qualitative research while attempts to answer the second and third questions are examples of quantitative research.[13]

Quantitative research in criminal justice explores the causes and consequences of crime and crime related processes and procedures. Quantitative criminal justice research might ask questions such as: What relationship exists between the age structure of a society and the rate and types of criminal behavior? What affect does increased police surveillance have on the rate of crime in a neighborhood? What consequences follow from the abolition of plea bargaining? or What affect do habitual offender statutes have on the crime rate? On the other hand, qualitative research is primarily descriptive. Its objective is to explore, clarify, and describe the characteristics of a social phenomenon. Qualitative research in criminal justice might ask: What are the characteristics of the inmate social system? What forms does serial homicide take? How does female criminal activity differ from the criminal behavior of males? or How does a parole officer actually supervise his/her clients?

This chapter outlines the methods and purposes of qualitative research in criminal justice. The difference between quantitative and qualitative research is "ideal-typical": when a researcher conducts a study, usually some combination of both qualitative and quantitative methodology is used. Only in the ideal or the abstract are the two methods completely different. For example, if you are conducting research in an effort to describe how a parole officer actually supervises his/her clients, you are also interested in offering some explanation for his/her behavior. Likewise, if I am trying to determine the affect an habitual offender statute has on the crime rate, I have an interest in describing, as well as explaining, this relationship. The differences are a matter of emphasis — as far as research questions are concerned.

Perhaps, the most important distinction between qualitative and quantitative research is that the research question determines the research design — specifically, the data collection procedures. Quantitative research attempts to explain and generalize. Qualitative research seeks in-depth, detailed information which, though not necessarily generalizable, allows for an as complete as possible understanding of the phenomenon. Quantitative research has generally relied on the experimental, quasi-experimental, and survey research designs. Qualitative research has relied primarily on participant observational studies, the case study and the survey. Since the case study and survey research have been covered, this chapter will concentrate on the forms of participant observation.

PARTICIPANT OBSERVATION

"It . . . is my belief that any group of persons — prisoners, primitives, pilots, or patients — develop a life of their own that becomes meaningful, reasonable, and normal once you get close to it, and that a good way to learn about any of these worlds is to submit oneself in the company of the members to the daily round of petty contingencies to which they are subject."[9]

Participant observation is the approach which gathers the most detailed and descriptive information. It is often called field research, and involves **participant observation**: being in, around, or near a social setting, situation and/or group of people for the purpose of describing and understanding the situation and the behaviors which take place in it.[13] This means that the investigator goes to the actual area in which a group of people live or the area where certain behaviors occur and studies the people or the behavior in a natural setting or environment. It involves getting physically, socially, and sometimes emotionally close to a group of people so that their life, their behavior becomes "meaningful, reasonable, and normal . . ."[9]

This method of research has a lengthy tradition, especially in Anthropology. Margaret Mead's pioneering work during the 1930s when she studied three separate cultures in New Guinea is an example of participant observation. She actually traveled to New Guinea and lived within these cultures. Even earlier, in the 1800s, Max Weber advanced his ideas on what he called **interpretive understanding** (Verstehen). Verstehen is subjective understanding of an activity which is identical or similar to the understanding of the actor(s) under study. Weber believed that this was only possible if the researcher could place himself/herself in the place of the individual under study and view the behavior from the actor's perspective.[7] The concept of **interpretive understanding** is central to participant observation. The assumption is that only people who are actually involved in some behavior can truly understand it. Therefore, the social scientist must try to see and interpret the world as much as possible from the perspective of the actor. Participant observation: (1) requires direct contact with the individuals under study, (2) requires that the researcher go into the social setting of the individuals under study, and (3) takes place in social settings that are relatively natural and normal for the subjects under study.[14] These strategies get the researcher into the natural environment of a group or the natural environment of the activities under study. The researcher is in direct contact with the research subjects. This method of study increases the researcher's empathy with his/her subjects and enhances his/her ability to adopt their perspective and understanding. This method of research is ". . . the most directly involving and therefore the most intimate and morally hazardous method of social research. It is precisely because it is the most penetrating of strategies, the most close and telling mode of gathering information, that it raises difficult social and moral questions . . ."[13] Some of these social and moral questions will become evident as we discuss the various types of participant observation and the advantages and disadvantages of each.

Complete Participant

The first form of participant observation is the **complete participant** or, what is sometimes called the unknown observer. This method of data collection places the researcher in a role similar to that of "spy" or "undercover detective." The investigator takes on a role in the group under study and pretends to be a "true" member while secretly studying the members of the group. For example, a researcher might take a job as a correctional counselor at a state reformatory for the purpose of studying correctional officers. Similarly, a researcher might join a police force or a juvenile gang to study and understand these groups.

Complete participation as a strategy may be the best way to learn the details of the life and behavior of a group. The researcher, disguised as a member of the group, is privy to the information of an accepted member of the group—an insider. Consequently, she or he can learn about aspects of group life that might otherwise be missed. For example, in *Asylums,* Erving Goffman describes in intimate detail the "underlife" of a total institution. His very detailed, vividly descriptive work on the behaviors of mental patients and staff is based on data gathered while a complete participant in the role of assistant to the athletic director at St. Elizabeth's Hospital. If he had been known as a researcher, his access to information may have been limited since many of the activities he observered were contrary to the rules and formal requirements of the institution. Similarly, a graduate student studied and reported on the Church of Satan by joining a group of Satanists, feigning conversion, and eventually becoming the official church historian. Because of his position in the church, he was able to learn details about rituals and members that would not be open to outsiders.[1]

The disadvantages of complete participation are mainly issues of morality and objectivity. When the results of this type of research are presented, typically the names of the subjects, the place of observation and any identifying criteria of the subjects, place, and group are withheld. However, the question of the morality of studying a group of people without their knowledge or permission still remains. Kai T. Erikson has assessed and commented on the ethics of participant observation and argues that it compromises both the researcher and the subjects under study. Erikson believes that participant observation may injure subjects in ways that cannot be anticipated nor compensated for after the fact. Since the researcher is not familiar with the group upon entry, the risk of unintended harm is great. Even the rationale of risking harm to subjects for social and scientific benefit is problematic since the subjects have not consented to be studied. Erikson compares complete participation to a " . . . physician who carries out medical experiments on human subjects without their consent."[6]

Complete participation may also be similar to "entrapment." When the investigator finally leaves the group and/or reveals his/her identity, members of the group may feel like they have been "set-up" or misled by the researcher. They may have bitter feelings because of this deception and feel that the investigator is a "traitor." These ethical questions can only be addressed by researchers themselves, using a set of professional ethics and standards that are objective in nature.

While complete participant studies are not numerous, they do generate much interest and controversy. Those who use this method of data collection need to be prepared to justify its selection over other forms of qualitative data collection. Richard Harris in *The Police Academy: An Inside View*[10] discusses the problems he faced in trying to select a method of data collection. His initial decision to tell police academy recruits that he was a researcher was changed to a complete participant role because the academy officers thought it might "scare recruits." Later on, when it became apparent that he was being treated differently by the administrators, and because of certain logistical problems, (i.e., not being able to issue him a numbered badge), his identity was threatened. At this point, he had to expose his position as a researcher and admit to the deception. Harris was lucky because the other police recruits had suspected something was going on and so were not completely surprised. However, many times people resent being deceived because their trust has been violated and they feel silly about letting someone "put one over on them." If the recruits in Harris' study has been angered or offended by his deception, it could have made his research efforts much more difficult — if not impossible.

In addition to the ethical issues raised by complete participation, there are other disadvantages. First, the role in the group that is played by the researcher naturally restricts his or her activity and so limits his or her ability to move about freely and observe. For example, a complete observer who secretly assumes the role of a police officer is not free to move about the police station observing interactions and interviewing police officers and suspects. Instead, he or she must perform the regular occupational duties of a police officer which necessarily restrict his or her mobility and the specific types of police activities which can be observed. Similarly, as an accepted yet disguised member of a group, a researcher is limited to questioning only those matters appropriate to the role he or she is playing. Too many questions about matters outside the role or about matters that should be known to group members who assume the role will raise suspicion.

A complete observer is also limited in his or her ability to immediately record observations. True group members do not carry tape recorders, video equipment, or note pads with them to record the daily life of the group. The result is that more dependence on memory is required and loss of information is possible. Complete participants may also be so self-conscious about revealing their true identity that their ability to perform their role and collect data is hampered. Finally, the opposite may occur, that is, complete participants may become so involved in their role and so committed to the group and subjects under study that they can no longer be objective. This problem is called "going native" and is an increasingly potential problem as researchers in the complete participant role spend more time in their disguise and become more involved with the group and its members. When a researcher "goes native," she/he loses objectivity because they have gotten so close to group members and group values that they **truly** become group members and are no longer in a deceptive role. For example, a researcher might attempt to study abused women while posing as a victim of spouse abuse in a shelter for battered women. While pretending to be a victim, she may get close to abused women and come to an empathetic understanding of their position and behaviors. However, if this identification becomes so strong that the researcher begins to react — without pretense — to counselors and other women in the shelter as if she had been abused, she has lost some objectivity. If she comes to adopt — without pretense — the attitudes and behaviors of abused women toward the police, men, the law, and workers in the shelter, she has "gone native." Her "make believe" role has become real and she is reacting subjectively rather than objectively. She has become so involved in her role that she cannot critically analyze it. George Kirkham who became a police officer in an attempt to understand the police and their problems[11] is an example of an academic researcher who "went native." Kirkham believes that one must be a policeman to understand the problems they face and stated that a "criminologist would not know a criminal if one bit him on the ass" — not an objective statement.

Participant as Observer

The participant as observer is similar to the complete participant role yet significantly different since the subjects know the researcher's true identity and purpose. The researcher may then observe and investigate both formally and informally. For example, a participant as observer may work in a correctional facility as a caseworker but his/her identity as a researcher is known by other workers in the facility. She/he may then be able to ask questions more freely and to be involved in more varied activities in the correctional facility without fear of being exposed (as is the case with the complete participant). This method was utilized by Richard McCleary in his study of parole: *Dangerous Men: The Sociology of Parole.*[15] McCleary accompanied several parole officers while they performed their field duties. The officers knew he was a researcher and not a parole officer. Because they knew of his research and of him, they were not bothered by his presence, in fact, as McCleary states ". . . in most cases, the PO's (parole officers) were happy to have some company in the field." While it was not the experience of McCleary, a researcher as participant observer may be viewed with caution, and possibly suspicion, by members of the group. However, over time, as the participant observer comes to be accepted by the group, the uneasiness of the subjects will disappear as trust and friendliness develop.

The major advantage of the participant as observer role is that it does not generate the ethical dilemma posed by the complete participant role. However, if the participant as observer is not accepted by the group and the initial mistrust and uneasiness is not overcome, the quality of information may be less than that gathered through complete participation. The participant as observer must also be aware that his or her presence may alter the behavior of those under study. Every attempt must be made to minimize this intrusion. Finally, the participant as observer must also be aware of commitment to the group under study. It is possible for the participant as observer to develop strong allegiances to groups under study, to "go native," and lose objectivity.

Observer as Participant

This method of data collection utilizes more formal observation techniques than the previous two methods. The observer as participant role utilizes the interview as a means of data collection. The observation and interaction are more formal and structured. The limited contact with the subjects reduces the chances of "going native" and losing objectivity. Additionally, an advantage is that notes may be taken and behaviors recorded openly. Detail may be easily retained. This method has disadvantages since it increases the likelihood of being misunderstood by and/or misunderstanding the individuals under study due to the minimal level of contact. For example, many researchers will be misidentified or misunderstood by the inmates who are their research subjects. Peter Lewis,[12] who studied inmates on death row in Florida, has told of his experiences as an interviewer. When he began his interviews, one of his first subjects was a child molester who was detested by all other inmates on death row. Since Mr. Lewis was introducing himself to each inmate individually at the beginning of the interview, none of the inmates knew who he was. Because of his dress and the restriction of access to death row for most outsiders, the inmates assumed he was an attorney who was attempting to help the child molester. The day after his interview with the child molester when he returned to death row to conduct another interview, the death row inmates were very angry with him. They cursed, spit, threw things at him, and generally caused quite a commotion until they were told about his true status and intentions. Many researchers have similar, though less extreme, examples of misconceptions held by their subjects. If they are clarified in time, their effect can be eliminated. If not, they can ruin an otherwise sound research project. The limited time the observer spends with the group and, the limited members she/he has contact with can reduce acceptance by the group and so that the atmosphere in which the interviews are conducted may be uneasy and the responses of the subjects less open.

Complete Observer

This method of data collection completely removes the researcher from direct interaction with his or her subjects. Usually the researcher attempts to observe the group in ways so that they will not know they are being observed or studied. For example, observing the behavior of sex offenders in a therapy group through a one-way mirror or systematically eavesdropping on the counselling sessions through hidden tape recorders might be two strategies. Another method could be similar to one used by Leonard Bickman and Helen Helwig[3] in a study of bystander reporting of crime. Bickman and Helwig set-up a field experiment in which they varied the anonymity of bystanders and the rewards for reporting and then measured the levels of reporting of a staged shoplifting incident. Subjects were interviewed by a confederate surveyor about shoplifting. After the interview, the confederate surveyor told them that she/he had heard that either (a) the store publicized those who reported incidents or did not, and that (b) the store either did or did not provide a reward for reports of shoplifting. What they found was that anonymity and reward had no effect. Instead, those shoppers who told the confederate surveyor that they would report a shoplifting incident if they saw it, did and those who reported they would not, did not.

The advantages to this form of data collection are that it has the least probability of the researcher "going native" and the least probability of influencing the subjects' behaviors through the presence of an observer. However, with these advantages which come from greater distance from and limited interaction with individuals under study come disadvantages.

TABLE 9.1

SUMMARY OF THE ADVANTAGES AND DISADVANTAGES
OF FORMS OF PARTICIPANT OBSERVATION

	Advantages	*Disadvantages*
Complete Participation	Detailed information as an "insider" No change in subjects' behavior	Activity and questions limited Field note taking restricted, much dependence on memory May be role self-consciousness Greatest probability of "going native" Ethical dilemmas
Participant Observer	Questions and movement not restricted by role playing Avoid ethical questions concerning subjects May openly record field data— less reliance on memory No role self-consciousness	Success of project dependent on gaining trust and acceptance of subjects Information may be limited due to "outsider" status Some probability of "going native"
Observer as Participant	Avoid ethical concerns No role self-consciousness Openly record observations Questions not restricted by role Lesser probability of "going native"	Contact with fewer subjects Very dependent on trust and rapport with subjects Limited ability to clarify through repeated questioning & observation Information less complete and detailed
Complete Observer	Subjects behavior not altered by observation Little probability of "going native" Openly record observation No role self-consciousness	Ethical considerations great Limited chance to clarify through repeated observation on questioning Less information and less detailed information

First, greater distance from the subjects decreases the researcher's ability to completely understand the social life he or she is studying. Statements and behaviors may be misperceived and misunderstood and the researcher has no mechanism for direct clarification. Similarly, the **ethical** issue of subject consent is also present, especially when clandestine methods of observation such as hidden microphones and video and recording equipment are utilized. Like the complete participant role, studies which use this methodology rely on subject deception. The justification for this is that if the subjects knew they were being studied, their behavior would change. However, many researchers disagree with this position and contend that subjects must have the right to refuse to be studied. The concern is that without their knowledge, subjects are being used. This is a violation of trust and fairness. If the subjects discover the deception they may resent the intrusion into their lives. Likewise, the discovery of deception may have short and long term consequences for the subjects. How would you feel, if (as some of the subjects in the Bickman and Helwig experiment did) you found out that your non-reporting of a shoplifting had been observed? Or, that the shoplifting incident you reported had been staged? Would you complain to the store manager? What would you do the next time you saw a shoplifting?

By this time, it should be obvious that each method of participant observation is different and each has its own unique set of advantages and disadvantages. Table 9.1 summarizes these advantages and disadvantages. The selection of a qualitative method for data collection should be based on three criteria: (1) the type of data sought, (2) the feasibility of using a specific method, and (3) ethical considerations, especially the risk of harm to the subjects. No one method is perfect, nor is any one method applicable to all needs for data collection. The method must be adjusted to meet the needs of the research and the subjects.

SELECTING A SETTING AND GAINING ENTREE INTO THE SETTING

Much of the available literature on participant observation provides little guidance on the fundamentals of choosing and entering a setting. This is probably because the best means to select a setting and gain permission to enter the setting are determined by the specific situation. However, there are some general guidelines which can be followed in an effort to enhance the success of the selection and entree process.

Locating the Setting

Selecting the setting in which a researcher collects qualitative data is an important and difficult task. First, the researcher must know some general characteristics of the subjects and the setting. Second, the acceptability of the setting is determined with three criterion in mind:

1. **Suitability:** Does the site meet the data collection needs of the researchers?

2. **Feasibility:** Does the site provide data that can be collected within the researcher's resource limitations (time, money, skills)?
3. **Suitable Tactics:** Does the site provide the researcher with available data collection options which are feasible? [18]

Information on the setting may be gathered through a variety of means: surveying documents and newspapers, phone calls, in-person interviews, or on site assessments. At times, it may be necessary to assess several settings before finding the appropriate or at least the most appropriate location. This is essential to the investigator's ability to gather **good** qualitative data. The setting from which the respondents are selected and the setting in which the observation takes place will greatly influence the quality of the collected data as well as the specific data collection techniques used by the researcher. For example, respondents who are incarcerated offenders may be more hesitant to participate or may attempt to manipulate and "con" a naive interviewer. Likewise, care must be taken to select an interview setting in which the inmates are comfortable, and feel free to speak without officers or administrators overhearing the conversation.

Gaining Entree

The selection of a setting will usually entail obtaining permission from someone in authority to enter the setting and conduct the research. The perfect setting may be found, but if permission to enter cannot be obtained, the setting must be reselected. Several general guidelines can be followed to obtain entree.

1. Always obtain permission from someone in authority to enter a setting. An investigator should never enter a setting without permission. If a researcher tries to collect information without permission, she/he can be held legally responsible for any problems created in the group or organization because of the intrusion. Likewise, she/he can be sued for violation of privacy by both the subjects and the authority which was bypassed.
2. Direct contact with the person of authority or contact with a lower level individual who can approach the top authority are both frequently used tactics. Which one an investigator elects to use will depend on the situation, and more specifically the approachability and availability of those in control.
3. Honesty in describing research objectives and methods is important. The researcher should identify himself or herself along with the spon-

soring agency or organizational affiliation. The research objectives and methodology should be clearly and honestly outlined. An important point that must be remembered is that permission for entree into a field setting will depend upon the value which those in authority place on the research project. The research must be worthwhile to them as well as the investigator. Therefore, delineating the benefits that could follow from the project for the organization, offers to include areas of interest to those in authority, and a willingness to provide feedback in the form of research findings are strategies which may make entree easier and which should not significantly affect the objectivity of the study.

4. The researcher must be prepared to negotiate the conditions of entree and to abide by conditions of entree which may be established. The authorizing agent may fear publicity, may feel that the research is useless, and may question the qualifications of the investigator or the investigator's affiliation. The researcher must be prepared to negotiate the requirements of entree to suit the orientation of the host organization or group. Similarly, conditions of entree may be set. Every group or organization has regulations and schedules. The researcher must be prepared to negotiate a research agreement which will not interfere with the regular daily operations of individuals in the setting. The researcher must be prepared to provide evidence of the unobtrusive, confidential, and anonymous nature of his or her research project. Once these conditions have been set they must not be violated.

5. Finally, the investigator must be continually aware of the fact that the quality of relations established and maintained with both the host and subjects will determine the quality and success of the research project. Amicable relations should be a continual objective — good relations are not just a requirement for entree but a continual requirement of the research process. The researcher is a "guest" and can be asked to leave the setting at any point in time.

RECORDING AND ANALYZING DATA

While participant observation may be ". . . similar to the interpretive procedures we make use of as we go about our everyday lives,"[19] there is one major difference. The researcher who elects to use qualitative methodology **explicitly** gathers, records, and analyzes information about a social setting. Rather than relying on memory and informal interpretation, the researcher attempts to formally record data in some form and to methodically analyze the information which had been collected.

Field Notes: Recording Data

Field notes ". . . provide the observer's 'raison d'etre.' "[13] Field notes contain the descriptive account of what a researcher has observed, or at least everything the researcher has observed and believes to be worth recording. Field notes are the recorded data which will be analyzed and from which conclusions will be drawn about the individuals under study. When utilizing a qualitative method of data collection, learning how to take field notes and what to record in them are major concerns. M.Q. Patton in *Qualitative Evaluation Methods*[17] has put forth some advice that could be formulated into the following guidelines:

- Do not trust future recall—try to record field experiences as immediately as possible after they occur.
- Get into the habit of regularly recording field experiences, set aside a time and place so that it becomes routine; **immediately** after the experience. Remember that field notes are descriptive as well as interpretive, include descriptions of events as well as thoughts, reactions, and interpretations of the observer.
- Be specific, include details of events which take place; include the date, time, where the observation took place, who was present, describe the setting, what interactions took place, and any other details to aide in the understanding of the experience.
- Include conversation, direct quotes if possible—informal conversation can give a wealth of information about members of a group.
- Include the researcher's feelings, reflections, judgments and reactions, the significance of the event to the researcher.
- Overall, keep in mind that the object of the research is to relay to others the experience of what it is like to be in the social setting, not as an observer but as a participant.

For the neophyte field researcher, field notes seem an overwhelming task. However, with practice the descriptive detail becomes easier to record. Additionally, technology has aided in the task of taking field notes. Tape recorders, dictaphones, typewriters, and photographic and video equipment have made field notes a less laborious process in some instances. Remember, you are the instrument, growing tired, hungry, etc. can affect the research data.

When taking field notes, the issue of how to take notes is as important as what to include in field notes. In some participant observation situations (i.e. the complete participant role), field notes must necessarily be taken secretly. If not, the role of the complete participant as a researcher and not a group member would be disclosed and the study, in all likelihood, terminated. Similarly, in other forms of participant observation the researcher must be careful not to make himself or herself too obvious by continuously taking notes or utilizing tape recording, photographic or video equipment. What must be kept in mind is the interactive nature of participant observation. In any role, the researcher becomes an element of the social setting and can influence the actors in that setting and alter their behaviors and their responses. The method of recording field notes must be selected using the criteria of **unobtrusiveness**. That is, it must have a negligent or minimal impact on the events or responses the researcher is attempting to observe and record.

Analyzing the Data

Qualitative data are attractive. They provide detailed, colorful, specific, experiential data for analysis. However, collecting and especially, analyzing the data can be a time consuming, laborious, and frustrating experience. First, a wealth of information must be meticulously recorded and then transferred to some useable form for analysis. the amount of data may present an overload for the researcher and the time to transcribe interviews and decipher field notes may be extensive.

Once the data is in a useable form an additional, though not insurmountable, problem exists for the researcher. Few guidelines for analysis exist. For quantitative data, there are clear conventions the researcher can use. However, the analyst faced with a bank of qualitative data has very few guidelines for protection against self delusion, let alone the presentation of " 'unreliable' or 'invalid' conclusions . . ."[16] The task, however unstructured, is not insurmountable.

Schatzman and Strauss[18] suggest that the analytic process begins with the data recording process. Researchers need to analyze and assess the process while in their participant observation roles so that they can shift their data collection emphasis to important events and settings as well as to clarify and/or key into significant data. Schatzman and Strauss[18] posit the discovery of **classes** (categories) of objects, people, events, and settings and the **properties** which characterize them as the primary objective of qualitative analysis. Through this process **linkages,** relationships or connections between the categories of phenomenon will emerge. Similarly, Lofland[13] suggests there are six general categories of phenomena the participant observer attempts to understand. These are:

1. **Acts.** Action in a situation that is temporarily brief, consuming only a few seconds, minutes, or hours.
2. **Activities.** Action in a setting of more major duration — days, weeks, months — constituting significant elements of the persons' involvements.
3. **Meanings.** The verbal productions of participants that define and direct action.
4. **Participation.** Persons' holistic involvement in, or adaptation to, a situation or setting under study.
5. **Relationships.** Interrelationships among several persons considered simultaneously.
6. **Settings.** The entire setting under study conceived as the unit of analysis.

The participant observer then is attuned to recording and classifying data into these categories. The task becomes more structured and directed because the questions to be answered are given focus. Rather than asking "What are the characteristics of this social group or event?" the question becomes: "What are the characteristics of acts, activities, meanings, participation, relationships, and settings, the forms they assume, the variations they display."[13] For example, what sorts of exchanges go on between members of the group? Who addresses whom? How do they behave toward one another? Do their actions suggest statuses in the group? A stratification hierarchy? What activities do the members engage in? What significance do the activities have? Who can participate in what activities with whom? How do settings determine the types of activities? or Are there some activities that can take place anywhere while others may only take place in specific settings? These types of questions give the study more focus. They direct the researcher's attention to important elements of group life. This direction reduces the uncertainty about what to observe.

Lofland[13] also suggests that the analysis of each unit of group life may be either static or phase. **Static analysis** attempts to describe social phenomenon at one point in time — like a photograph. **Phase analysis** seeks to record social phenomenon and processes over time — like a movie. Giallombardo's[8] study of women's roles in prison: snitches, squares, rap buddies, honeys, connects, boosters, penitentiary turnouts, lesbians, punks — to name a few — was a static analysis of a women's prison. These roles represented a woman's participation in the prison subculture and interaction patterns with staff and inmates. The roles were identified and described, a photograph, of sorts, was taken of the informal social organization of a woman's prison at that point in time. The longitudinal interview study by Buffum[4] in which he sought to determine rates of use of aftercare facilities, the problems of ex-offenders following release, the criminal activity of ex-offenders and the **process** of agency use is an example of a **phase analysis.** Likewise, Harris's[10] work on the police academy included phase analysis in his description of the nature and process of the depersonalization of police recruits. The form of the analysis — phase or static — like the form of participant observation, is selected with specific research needs in mind.

As the participant observer collects data, certain categories of acts, actions, participants, and relationships will become clear. The content of the field notes can then be classified to see if the hypothesized categories "fit" all the data. Content analysis of interviews and/or written material from subjects may be analyzed. Case studies may be developed as examples which best represent an observed characteristic of some unit of the social setting. All in all, the process is tedious, and involves ordering and reordering categories and criteria for classification. It will, in all likelihood, demand as much time, if not more, than the data collection procedure. The result however, will be in-depth insights into social settings and human behavior.

INTERVIEWING

One of the methods of participant observation — observer as participant — deserves further discussion. Within this form of qualitative data collection the researcher utilizes interviews with subjects to gather information. While on the surface, this may appear to be one of the easier and less problematic modes of participant observation, it is a complicated process which requires skill and attentiveness from the researcher.

During an interview the object is to collect data on human behavior through the use of structured, methodical "talks" with individuals. The structure of these "talks" imposes constraints on the discussion such as, questions asked, ordering of questions, and place of the interview which serve to improve the accuracy of the information gathered.[14]

The assumption is that those involved in a social setting have the best information about that setting and can be tapped as an important source of information. Through interviewing a researcher can discover information that cannot be observed by attempting to discover what is on an individual's mind, the subjective perspective of the person being interviewed.

According to Patton[17] there are three basic approaches to interviewing.

1. **Informal Conversational Interview:** This format uses spontaneous questions, asked informally in the context of an ongoing participant observation study. The questions are not predetermined and vary with the subject and setting.

   Advantages: This form of interview allows the researcher the greatest flexibility and responsiveness to respondent differences and situational changes. It is also less threatening to the respondent because of its informal nature.

   Disadvantages: The data collected from each subject may differ making it more difficult to analyze. It takes longer to collect systematic information when this method is utilized so an extended period of interviewing in the field setting is required. This method may be easily affected by the conversational and interviewing style and skills of the interviewer.

2. **General Interview Guide Approach:** This interview format is more formal than the conversational interview. The interviewer has a series of issues which have been selected prior to the interview situation. They have no specific ordering, but are used as a checklist of topics to be covered.

   Advantages: The information gathered through this method is similar for each respondent making it easier to analyze. The interviewing, while more systematic, still allows the interviewer the flexibility to probe and explore responses when necessary. This interview is more efficient because the interviewer has some plan and utilizes limited interview time more efficiently than when the interview is less structured.

   Disadvantages: The data, though more structured, are still conversational and informal and may be difficult to analyze. Though not as extensive as with the conversation interview, this interview is also easily influenced by the conversational and interviewing skills of the interviewer.

3. **Standardized Open-Ended Interview:** This form of interview consists of a set of pre-established, carefully worded questions arranged

in a specific order. The wording and ordering are developed with the intent of obtaining comparable responses from each subject.

Advantages: The standardized interview minimizes variation in responses making them more comparable and easier to analyze. This form of interview is the best and most efficient form to use when interviews are limited to one per subject and when the time for each interview and/or the series of interviews is limited. There is also less potential for influences from the interviewer conversational style and interviewing techniques.

Disadvantages: The interviewer's flexibility and so, ability to probe, explore, and expand on responses is limited. This may increase the chance that responses may be incomplete or misinterpreted. Likewise, it reduces the interviewer's opportunity to take into account individual differences and variations in circumstances. This may diminish the rapport between the interviewer and subject and/or the quality of the responses.

The fundamental principle to keep in mind is that the interview should provide a structure in which the respondents can express their own feelings and experiences in their own terms. The method of interviewing must meet the needs of the respondent as well as research needs. If respondents are not given a comfortable framework for response, the information gathered through the interviews will not be of good quality or quantity. Two conventions govern the role of the interviewer in his or her attempt to elicit information from respondents: **equality** and **comparability.**[17] The interview situation must be one in which the interviewer and respondent perceive of each as equal in status for the duration of the interview. The structure must also minimize the specific, concrete circumstances of the exchange so that each interview is similar to another. The intrusion of personalities must be minimized.

Lastly, the question of **who** and how **many** to interview remains. Obviously, the **number** of respondents will also be determined by the nature of the information sought. For example, if a researcher is interested in a warden's interpretation of an incident of collective violence in his or her institution, **an** interview with **a** warden may be sufficient. However, if the objective is to obtain the reaction of the **average** inmate in the institution to the riot then interviews with **several** inmates may be necessary to ensure **representativeness** and **generalizability.**

Who to interview will be determined by the type of information sought as well as time, money, and the availability of subjects. Subjects may be interviewed as **informants** or **respondents.**[14] **Informants** are viewed as surrogate observers, **respondents** are interviewed when information on the individual subject is of interest. In either case, care must be taken to consider the subject's role in the social setting and how that role will affect their responses. A specialized form of informant interviewing is **elite interviewing.** In elite interviewing the investigator allows, if not encourages, the respondent to teach him or her about the situation, or to seemingly take the lead in structuring the interview. The interview is less standardized, and more exploratory than non-elite interviews. In the elite interview, not all persons are equal. In fact, the information from the respondent in an elite interview is used for reinterpretation, reassessment, and reformulation of research data and information.[5]

CONCLUSION

Qualitative data gathered through participant observation can provide insightful, detailed information about human behavior. However simplistic participant observation may seem at first glance, or however similar it may seem to be to observational strategies we use in our everyday life, it is a complicated and timely methodology which requires a great deal of discretion on the part of the investigator. Because participant observation has not been used extensively in the social sciences — especially in criminal justice research there are few specific guidelines for an investigator to follow. As discussed in this chapter, there are a number of methods of data collection and analysis, each with advantages and disadvantages. The important criterion for a researcher to use in selecting among the methodologies are: research needs, and methodology feasibility. The method must be selected with the research objectives and the feasibility of applying the methodology in mind. There is no **perfect** qualitative method. There are only methods which are better suited for **some research interests** in **some situations.** The objective is to structure the methodology so that the nature and quality of information gathered will meet the established research needs. The method should never structure the form of the research question.

KEY TERMS

Participant Observation
Complete Participant

"Go Native"
Observer as Participant
Complete Observer
Unobtrusiveness
Classes, Properties, Linkages
Acts, Activities, Meanings, Participation, Relationships, Settings
Static Analysis
Phase Analysis
Informal Conversational Interview
General Interview Guide
Standardized Open-Ended Interview
Equality
Comparability
Elite Interviewing

STUDY GUIDE

1. What is participant observation? How is it related to the concept of interpretive understanding?
2. How is the complete participant like an undercover cop?
3. What ethical concerns have been raised about complete participation?
4. What is "going native"? How is it a problem for each form of participant observation?
5. Keeping the advantages and disadvantages of each form of participation in mind, try to think of a research project best suited for each form.
6. What impact would knowing you have been deceived by a researcher have on you? How would it be different if it were a complete participant versus a complete observer, if at all?
7. Assume you would like to be an observer as participant in your local police department. What strategies, guidelines would you use to gain entree and make your research arrangements?
8. Describe the guidelines for recording field notes.
9. According to Lofland, what six categories of behavior does a participant observer attempt to understand? Think of some behaviors of your own peer group that would fall into each category.
10. Discuss the advantages and disadvantages of the three approaches to interviewing.

11. What criteria are utilized to decide which interview form to use, who to interview, and how many to interview?
12. How is elite interviewing different from other types of interviewing?

REFERENCES

1. Babbie, Earl: *The Practice of Social Research,* 3rd Ed. (Belmont, California: Wadsworth, 1983).
2. Benny, Mark and Hughes, Everett C.: "Of sociology and the interview," *American Journal of Sociology* 62 (1956) 137-142.
3. Bickman, Leonard and Helwig, Helen: Bystander reporting of a crime: The impact of incentives, *Criminology* 17 (1979) 283-300.
4. Buffum, Peter C.: The Philadelphia aftercase survey: A summary report, *The Prison Journal* 56 (1976) 3-24.
5. Dexter, Lewis A.: *Elite and Specialized Interviewing* (Evanston: Northwestern University Press, 1970).
6. Erikson, Kai T.: A comment on disguised observation in sociology, *Social Problems* 14 (1967) 366-373.
7. Freund, Julien: *The Sociology of Max Weber,* (New York: Vintage Books, 1969).
8. Giallombardo, Rose: Social roles in a prison for women, *Social Problems* 13 (1966) 268-288.
9. Goffman, Erving: *Asylums,* (Garden City, New York: Anchor Books, 1961).
10. Harris, Richard N.: *The Police Academy An Inside View,* New York: John Wiley & Sons, 1973).
11. Kirkham, George L.: *Signal Zero: The Professor Who Became a Street Cop,* (Philadelphia: Lippincott, 1976).
12. Lewis, Peter W. and Peoples, Kenneth D.: *The Supreme Court and the Criminal Process — Cases and Comments,* (Philadelphia: W.B. Saunders, 1978).
13. Lofland, John: *Analyzing Social Settings,* (Belmont, California: Wadsworth, 1971).
14. McCall, George J.: *Observing the Law: Field Methods in the Study of Crime and the Criminal Justice System,* (New York: Free Press, 1978).
15. McCleary, Richard: *Dangerous Men, The Sociology of Parole,* (Beverly Hills, California: Sage, 1978).
16. Miles, Matthew B.: Qualitative data as an attractive nuisance: The problem of analysis, *Administrative Science Quarterly* (1979) 590-601.
17. Patton, Michael Quinn: *Qualitative Evaluation Methods,* (Beverly Hills: Sage, 1980).
18. Schatzman, Leonard and Strauss, Anselm L.: *Field Research, Strategies for a Natural Sociology,* (Englewood Cliffs, NJ: Prentice-Hall, 1973).
19. Van Maanen, John: Reclaiming qualitative methods for organizational research: A preface, *Administrative Science Quarterly* 24 (1979) 520-526.

CHAPTER TEN

SCALING

OFTEN, researchers attempt to gauge the degree, strength, or amount of phenomenon under study. In order to accomplish this task in a quantitative fashion, it is necessary to reduce the phenomenon to a numerical scale. In this chapter, we introduce the concept of scaling and the ways in which a scale can be constructed. Scaling is also related to concepts such as levels of measurement (Chapter Two) and validity and reliability (Chapter Four). We also give special attention to the use of scales developed by researchers to measure the severity of crime and client performance under probation or parole supervision.

Scales are techniques which attempt to develop measurements of a concept. They usually involve the construction of several elements or questions which are assigned a numerical value. The score on each item is then added together to form a total score value. This single score then serves as an indication of the concept under analysis. In this manner, the scale combines several items (which measure different aspects of the concept) into a total score (which represents the total amount of the concept which is present). The researcher then has the option and the flexibility to examine each item on the scale individually and/or to conduct an analysis using the total score value.

CONCEPTS IN SCALING

There are several important issues which must be considered in the construction or use of a measurement scale. First, there is the question of face validity: the items included in the scale should, at face value, provide some measure of the concept under consideration. For example, in his study of the use of the death penalty in South Carolina, Paternoster[15] developed a basic scale which was designed to measure the heinousness of a homicide. He identified four factors which indicated the degree of seriousness or severity of the murder and assigned a value of one point if any of the following factors were present in the case: if the homicide involved strangers, if there were multiple victims, if there were multiple offenders, and if female victims were in evidence. Here, the researcher would review a case and scan for the presence of these factors; resulting in a score ranging from 0 to 4. Note that the items included in the scale do have face validity—they have a "common sense" ring to them in that they do provide an indication of the type of murders which are commonly held to be heinous. Again, the researcher now can analyze the cases according to the scale values on the individual items as well as the total score.

In addition, the items on a scale should be unidimensional. They should measure differing amounts of the same concept under consideration. Again, the Paternoster scale meets this requirement since each item relates to the heinousness of the murder. Unidimensionality is especially important when the researcher intends to combine each item on the scale to form a total score value. After all, if one item on the scale duplicated the concept measured by another item, the total value would be inaccurate. In other words, the researcher would not have the ability to analyze the total score value if unidimensionality were not present.

There is also the issue of internal validation: the relationship between the scale items and the total score value. The scores on each individual item on the scale should rank the cases in terms of the total score value. The key question is, "Does the total score value reflect the scoring patterns on the individual items?" Is there a consistent and clear pattern between the individual items and the total score? External validation refers to other indicators not included in the scale. Is there a relationship between other measures included in the study and the items included in the scale? For example, if you were collecting data on cases involving persons convicted of murder, are the items on the scale and the total score related to the decision of (and sentence imposed by) the court in the case? If the scale has both internal and external validity, the resulting measures are much more accurate in terms of its ability to measure the concept under study.

TYPES OF SCALES

Scales are not only used in research but also as a guide to decision making throughout the criminal justice system. Research has made an impact upon operations in different agencies. Measurement scales are used to help guide parole board decision making,[9,10] caseload management in probation and parole supervision,[5] bail release procedures,[6] and classification of inmates in prison.[3,11] Basically, these scales are prediction scales which are based upon an analysis of the performance (i.e., recidivism) of a group of subjects (i.e., parolees). The scale then indicates the risk factors associated with the behavior under study. The analysis of this type of scaling procedure is beyond the scope of this chapter. Instead, we will focus upon the use of scales which attempt to measure attitudes or a particular phenomenon (i.e., the severity of crime). The criminal justice researcher often uses scales which have been developed to measure certain items. For example, Brodsky and Smitherman[2] have compiled some 380 scales which have been used in studies on crime, law, delinquency, and corrections. Texts such as these should be consulted by researchers before they attempt an attitudinal study. It may not be necessary to construct a brand new scale to measure the concept under analysis.

However, the researcher must be aware of the fact that existing scales must be validated: that is, it must be demonstrated that the scale measures what it was designed to measure. It must also be reliable: upon repeated use, the scale should produce the same or similar results (see Chapter Four). Researchers and criminal justice officials often make the mistake of assuming that, since a scale has proven effective under one set of circumstances, it has universal application. For example, Wright, Clear, and Dickson[20] have demonstrated that probation and parole supervision instruments (designed to measure both the risk of recidivism posed by and the specific treatment needs of the client) are not universally applicable and that they must be carefully validated in each locale. They tested the Wisconsin scale with a sample of New York City probationers and determined that many of the variables contained in the instrument did not accurately predict risk in that situation. Therefore, existing scales must be utilized with caution.

Likert Scales

Likert scales are commonly associated with attitudinal questionnaires. The format of a Likert scale (named for Rensis Likert[13]) is familiar to persons who have responded to such studies. Basically, the subject is asked to respond to a series of statements and to indicate whether he/she "strongly agrees, agrees, is not sure, disagrees, or strongly disagrees"

TABLE 10.1

LIKERT SCALE: MEASUREMENT OF CONSERVATIVE ATTITUDES
TOWARD CRIME AND CRIMINALS

Directions: Answer the following questions and state the extent to which you either agree or disagree with the following statements. Use the following scale to indicate the extent of your agreement:

    1 = Strongly Disagree
    2 = Disagree
    3 = Uncertain
    4 = Agree
    5 = Strongly Agree

1. Most criminals know exactly what they are doing when they break the law.
2. The main reason why we have so much crime is because young people are not taught to respect authority.
3. Stiff sentences are necessary to show criminals that crime does not pay and to make sure that they don't commit crimes again.
4. Rehabilitating a criminal is just as important as making him/her pay for the crime.
5. The major goal of the criminal justice system should be to protect society from violent crime, communists and other politically disruptive people.
6. "The rich get richer and the poor get prison" is a fair way to characterize how our criminal "justice" system works.
7. If we really cared about crime victims, we would make sure that criminals were caught and given harsh punishments.

---

with the statement in question. In this manner, a Likert scale generally measures the intensity of feeling which the subject demonstrates. The items on the scale should be unambiguous: they should clearly reflect a definable opinion concerning the attitude under study. The items should be ordered in such a way that the total score indicates a high degree of the attitude in question (i.e., support for capital punishment). An example of a Likert scale is presented in Table 10.1.

    The purpose of this scale is to measure the extent of agreement with conservative attitudes and policies toward crime and criminals. This scale is a modification of a scale developed by Garrett and Matthews which was utilized in an analysis of the opinions of legislators on criminal justice policy.[4] The range of scale values is from 7 to 35. The higher the score, the more clearly the respondent is expressing a conservative attitude toward crime. However, notice that items 4 and 7 reflect liberal attitudes toward crime. These items serve as checks upon the responses of individuals. Persons who score high on the conservative scale should register a low score on these two scale items. Therefore, when a Likert scale is utilized, it is necessary to conduct an item analysis to determine which individual items correlate the highest with the total score value. The items which correlate in this manner are then selected to form the modified scale which then serves as the basis for analysis. The item analysis is not only applicable to the response check items (i.e., items 4 and 7) but to every item on the scale.

Utilized in this fashion, Likert scaling can provide an accurate method of gauging the intensity of attitudes toward a certain phenomenon.

Thurstone Scale

This type of scale is developed by judges. The judges are individuals who are surveyed and asked their opinion about the concept in question. For some reason, their opinions are considered to be expert. Their responses (usually in the form of some type of ranking) are then utilized to form a scale which measures the phenomenon under consideration. Miller[14] notes that the judges classify a number of statements ranging from most favorable to neutral to most favorable. This ranking system (usually consisting of 11 groups) has been set by the researcher in such a manner that the intervals between the groups are approximately equal. This is why the Thurstone scale is commonly known as an equal appearing intervals scale. The scale value of a statement included in the new scale is the median value which it has been assigned by the judges. Statements which have a broad spread of values assigned by the judges are dropped from the scale.

One disadvantage of this type of scale construction is that it would take a considerable amount of time, effort, and expense to generate a Thurstone scale. After all, the researcher must create the statements, group them, construct a sampling list of the judges, conduct a survey of the judges, analyze the results and then construct the scale. In short, the construction of a Thurstone scale is a survey research project in and of itself. Despite the vast amount of work posed by this procedure, it is used.

For example, Wolfgang, Figlio, Tracy, and Singer[19] conducted a national survey of crime severity. The purpose of the survey was to ascertain public attitudes about the severity of crime. They surveyed some 60,000 persons over the age of 18 in regard to their opinion about crime. This survey was conducted in conjunction with the National Crime Survey (see Chapter Four) in 1977. The procedure was relatively simple. The respondents were given the following description of a crime: "A person

TABLE 10.2

HOW DO PEOPLE RANK THE SEVERITY OF CRIME: THE TOP TEN
RANKINGS FROM *THE NATIONAL SURVEY OF CRIME SEVERITY*

Severity Score	Offense Description
72.1	A person plants a bomb in a public building. The bomb explodes and 20 people are killed.
52.8	A man forcibly rapes a woman. As a result of physical injuries, she dies.
47.8	A parent beats his young child with his fists. As a result, the child dies.
43.9	A person plants a bomb in a public building. The bomb explodes and one person is killed.
43.2	A person robs a victim at gunpoint. The victim struggles and is shot to death.
39.2	A man stabs his wife. As a result, she dies.
39.1	A factory knowingly gets rid of its waste in a way that pollutes the water supply of a city. As a result, 20 people die.
35.7	A person stabs a victim to death.
35.6	A person intentionally injures a victim. As a result, the victim dies.
33.8	A person runs a narcotic ring.

steals a bicycle parked on the street" and were told that the seriousness rating for this crime was 10. They were then provided with the descriptions of other crimes and were asked to rate them in comparison to the bicycle theft. Thus, if you considered a crime description to be twice as serious as bicycle theft, you would rate it as 20. Every respondent ranked 25 crimes and a total number of 204 crime descriptions were reviewed.

A summary of the responses are listed in Table 10.2 The severity score rankings were compiled from the ratings of the judges (respondents) and were developed through a complex weighting procedure. The top ten crime rankings listed in the table reveal that persons have different opinions concerning the severity of crime. These responses were also utilized to develop a scale to measure the severity of a crime which will be considered later.

Guttman Scale

Another commonly used method of scaling was developed by Guttman.[7] It is also known as scalogram analysis in that the researcher can determine if the attitude (or behavior) in question fits a certain, ordered response pattern. Typically, the items on the scale are placed in such a

TABLE 10.3

EXAMPLE OF A GUTTMAN SCALE:
SELF-REPORTED CRIME SURVEY

QUESTIONS:
Have you ever been:

SCALE SCORE:	Incarcerated?	Convicted?	Arrested?
3	Yes	Yes	Yes
2	No	Yes	Yes
1	No	No	Yes
0	No	No	No

manner that the overall response pattern can be predicted on the basis of the total score of the individual. The primary purpose of the scale is to determine if a "universe of attitude" statements in unidimensional — only those items which form a single dimension of the attitude (or behavior) are included in the scale.

Table 10.3 presents an example of a Guttman scale. Here, we are interested in conducting a self-report study of criminal behavior (see Chapter Four) and each respondent answered the three questions contained in the scale. The items on the scale are cumulative and affirmative answers to one question also result in positive answers to other questions on the scale. For example, if a person has been incarcerated, that person has also been arrested and convicted to that a "triangular" response pattern is evident.

Naturally, it is not so easy to construct a Guttman scale. Such an ideal response pattern is not usually present. It is necessary to calculate the coefficient of reproducibility in order to construct a Guttman scale. It is calculated in the following manner:

$$\text{Reproducibility} = 1 - \frac{\text{Number of errors}}{\text{Number of responses}}$$

"Errors" refer to those responses which fail to fit the triangular response pattern. Items which fail to fit the pattern should be discarded. For example, if we included the following statement to our hypothetical scale: "Have you ever been the victim of a crime?" this statement would be dropped because it is unrelated to the indicators of criminality which we have included in the scale. Victimization is not related to arrest, conviction, and incarceration. If the coefficient of reproducibility equals .90, unidimensionality is present and a Guttman scale exists. A Guttman scale is ordinal in nature and permits the use of some statistical analysis. However, one should not assume that a Guttman scale can be repeatedly used without specific attention to the nature of the respondent population and the attitude (or behavior) under consideration.[8]

POTENTIAL USES OF MEASUREMENT SCALES

No matter what the form of the scale, these measurement devices have a number of uses in criminal justice research. Here, we will consider the uses of two scales: the severity of crime scale developed by Wolfgang, Figlio, Tracy, and Singer[19] and the positive adjustment scale constructed by Seiter.[1]

Severity of Crime Scale

The severity of crime scale (see Table 10.4) was developed as a result of the National Survey of Crime Severity and it therefore reflects public sentiment about which crimes are most serious. It also represents a revision of an earlier attempt by Sellin and Wolfgang[16] to construct a crime severity index. The need for such a scale is rather obvious. If a researcher is primarily interested in gauging the severity of an offense, he/she has a few potential sources to make such a determination. You could consider the charge at arrest or conviction. The problem here is that the charge may not adequately reflect the events surrounding the crime (see Chapter Four) due to the fact that police may "overcharge" an individual at arrest and that the conviction offense may be complicated by "plea bargaining." Even the use of the UCR/FBI "crime index" (see Chapter Four) cannot solve this potential problem. The crime index offense may not adequately reflect the severity of the crime due to the fact that it: (1) fails to count multiple offenses, (2) does not differentiate between completed and attempted crimes, and (3) does not weigh crimes according to their severity.

A severity scale is one mechanism which can be used to solve these measurement problems. The researcher must have a description of the offense (normally provided in the police report or in the presentence investigation compiled by the probation officer). Using these data, the researcher can then ascertain the severity of the offense committed.

TABLE 10.4

SCALE OF OFFENSE SEVERITY:
THE NATIONAL SURVEY OF CRIME SEVERITY

Identification Number: _____

Effects of Event   I   T   D   (circle all that apply)

Component Scored	Number of Victims ×	Scale Weight =	Total
I Injury			
(a) Minor harm	_____	1.47	_____
(b) Treated and discharged	_____	8.53	_____
(c) Hospitalized	_____	11.98	_____
(d) Killed	_____	35.67	_____
II Forcible sex acts			
III Intimidation			
(a) Verbal or physical	_____	4.90	_____
(b) Weapon	_____	5.60	_____
IV Premises forcibly entered	_____	1.50	_____
V Motor vehicle stolen			
(a) Recovered	_____	4.46	_____
(b) Not recovered	_____	8.07	_____
VI Property theft/damage	_____	*	_____
		Total Score	_____

*$\log 10Y = .26776656 \log 10X$
    where Y = crime severity weight
          X = total dollar value of theft or damage

The seriousness scoring system listed in Table 10.4 consists of six basic elements surrounding a criminal event:

1. The number of victims who, during the event, received minor bodily injuries or were treated and discharged, hospitalized, or killed.
2. The number of victims of forcible sexual intercourse.
3. The presence of physical or verbal intimidation or intimidation by a dangerous weapon.
4. The number of premises forcibly entered.
5. The number of motor vehicles stolen and whether the vehicle was or was not recovered.
6. The total dollar amount of property loss during an event through theft and damage.

Specifically, the scale operates in the following manner. First, the criminal event must be classified in terms of the presence of I (injury), T (theft) and D (damage). It is possible to have seven different classifications of an event (I, T, D, IT, ID, TD, and ITD). On the scale scoring sheet, column 1 presents the offense components in the scale, column 2 refers to the number of victims involved, column 3 gives the scale weight for each event (developed via the survey), and column 4 then contains the total score for each given event. The figures in column 4 are then summed to obtain the final score. These items are very straightforward and there are few quirks in the application of this scale. However, the researcher must be careful to note that the scale is designed in such a way that a forcible sex act is considered to be always accomplished by intimidation. Therefore, any forcible sex act should also be scored in terms of the type of intimidation used by the assailant. Also, a motor vehicle theft is not included under item 6 since it has already been considered in item 5. Researchers should also note that the scale weight for property theft/damage (item 6) is rather complex and will require some special attention.

This scoring system has a number of potential research applications. The severity of an offense could be applied to such outcome measures as recidivism (see Chapter 11) and determining the severity of a criminal career. For example, Wilson[18] utilized the Sellin-Wolfgang scale in her analysis of Kentucky prisoners who were prosecuted and incarcerated under a "persistent felony offender" law. She used the scale to determine the severity of the current offense committed by the "PFO"s in order to ascertain the level of violence present. Among her conclusions were that 43 percent of the incarcerated PFOs had recently committed crimes which included some form of threatened or actual violence. Thus, this scale can be used in a number of ways to improve the manner in which criminological studies are conducted.

Positive Adjustment Scale

In Chapter Eleven, the problems in the measurement of recidivism rates are discussed. One of the basic problems with recidivism as an outcome measure is that it is strictly a negative indicator. Due to its very nature, recidivism does not consider any positive behavior which the client engages in. This was precisely the problem faced by Seiter[1] in his evaluation of halfway house program effectiveness. His basic premise was that the successful adjustment of an offender should not be judged

TABLE 10.5

POSITIVE ADJUSTMENT SCALE

DIRECTIONS: Assign one point for the attainment of any of the following adjustment criteria.

Employed, enrolled in school, or participating in a training program for more than 50 percent of the follow-up period.

Held any one job (or continued in educational or vocational program) for more than a six month period during the follow-up.

Attained vertical mobility in employment, educational, or vocational programs.

For the last half of the follow-up period, individual was self-supporting and supported any immediate family.

Individual shows stability in residency. Either lived in the same residence for more than six months or moved at the suggestion or with the agreement of the supervising officer.

Individual has avoided any critical incidents that show instability, immaturity, or inability to solve problems acceptably.

Attainment of financial stability. This is indicated by the individual living within his means, opening bank accounts or meeting debt payments.

Participation in self-improvement programs. These could be vocational, educational, group counseling, or alcohol or drug maintenance program.

Individual making satisfactory progress through probation period. This could be moving downward in levels of supervision or obtaining final release within the follow-up period.

No illegal activities on any available records during the follow-up period.

---

on the basis of his/her criminal behavior alone and that positive (or acceptable) behavior patterns should also be considered. Seiter then developed a two part scale which measured criminal behavior (in terms of a scale which corresponded to the Ohio legal code) and a measure of acceptable behavior patterns. Since we have already considered a measure of the severity of behavior, we will focus upon the "positive adjustment" segment of the Seiter scale.

Table 10.5 lists the elements of the positive adjustment scale. It is designed to provide some quantitative measure of "acceptable living patterns." The indicators are not designed as measures of success; rather they should be considered as an index of adjustment within the community. Its major emphasis is upon work or educational stability but other indicators of self-improvement (i.e., financial responsibility, parole or probation progress, absence of critical incidents or illegal activities) are also included. Therefore, the scale appears to have face validity: the qualities listed in the scale suggest stability, responsibility, maturity, and a general pattern of socially acceptable behavior.

Each item on the scale is weighted equally. Individuals receive one point as they qualify for each criterion. The positive adjustment score is the total number of criterion registered by the individual. The scoring range is from 0 through 10. Of course, the individual items as well as the total score value can be examined by researchers. The positive adjustment scale has been utilized in a number of studies; particularly in the evaluation of intensive supervision (Latessa[12]) and a prison drug/alcohol rehabilitation programs (Vito[17]). Its basic strength lies in its attempt to provide a positive measure of performance and a point of comparison to the traditionally negative measure of recidivism.

CONCLUSION

This chapter provided a basic overview of the major types of measurement scales (Likert, Thurstone, Guttman) and gave some specific attention to the measurement of crime severity and positive adjustment by clients in rehabilitation programs. The criminal justice researcher must be aware of these different forms and make use of existing scales when it is feasible to do so. The measurement of phenomena in a quantitative manner can facilitate and provide more accurate indicators of performance in the criminal justice system.

KEY TERMS

External validation
Face validity
Internal validation
Reproducibility
Unidimensional

STUDY GUIDE

1. Identify the key features of the Likert, Thurstone, and Guttman scales.
2. What was the purpose of the National Survey of Crime Severity?

3. Use the crime severity scale to compute a score for the following crime incident: A holdup man forces a husband and his wife to get out of their automobile. He shoots the husband, gun whips and rapes the wife (hospitalized) and leaves the automobile (recovered later). The husband dies as a result of the shooting.
4. What are the goals of the Positive Adjustment Scale?

REFERENCES

1. Allen, Harry E. and Seiter, Richard P.: The effectiveness of halfway houses: A reappraisal of a reappraisal. *Chitty's Law Journal* 24: 196-200, 1976.
2. Brodsky, Stanley L. and Smitherman, H. O'Neal: *Handbook of Scales for Research in Crime and Delinquency.* New York, Plenum, 1983.
3. Buchanan, Robert A., Whitlow, Karen L., and Austin, James: National evaluation of objective prison classification systems: The current state of the art. *Crime and Delinquency* 32: 272-290, 1986.
4. Cullen, Francis T., Bynum, Timothy S., Garrett, Kim, and Greene, Jack R.: Legislator ideology and criminal justice policy. In Fairchild, Erika S. and Webb, Vincent J. (Eds.): *The Politics of Crime and Criminal Justice.* Beverly Hills: Sage, 1985.
5. Eaglin, James B. and Lombard, Patricia A.: Statistical risk prediction as an aid to probation caseload classification. *Federal Probation* 45: 25-32, 1981.
6. Eskridge, Chris W.: *Pretrial Release Programming.* New York: Clark Boardman, 1983.
7. Guttman, Louis L.: A basis for scaling qualitative data. *American Sociological Review* 9: 139-150, 1944.
8. Hirschi, Travis and Selvin, Hanan C.: *Delinquency Research: An Appraisal of Analytic Methods.* New York: Free Press, 1967.
9. Hoffman, Peter B.: Screening for risk: A revised salient factor score (SFS/81). *Journal of Criminal Justice* 11: 539-547, 1983.
10. Hoffman, Peter B. and Adelberg, Sheldon: The salient factor score: A nontechnical overview. *Federal Probation* 45: 185-188, 1980.
11. Kane, Thomas R.: The validity of prison classification: An introduction to practical considerations and research issues. *Crime and Delinquency* 32: 367-390, 1986.
12. Latessa, Edward J.: Intensive diversion unit: An evaluation. In Price, Barbara R. and Baunach, Phyllis Jo (Eds.): *Criminal Justice Research: New Models and Findings.* Beverly Hills: Sage, 1980.
13. Likert, Rensis: A technique for the measurement of attitudes. *Archives Psychology,* No. 140, 1932.
14. Miller, Delbert C. (Ed.): *Handbook of Research Design and Social Measurement.* New York, McKay, 1977.
15. Paternoster, Raymond: Race of the victim and location of crime: The decision to seek the death penalty in South Carolina. *The Journal of Criminal Law and Criminology,* 74: 754-785, 1983.

16. Sellin, Thorsten and Wolfgang, Marvin E.: *The Measurement of Delinquency.* New York, John Wiley & Sons, 1964.

17. Vito, Gennaro F.: Does it work? Problems in the evaluation of a correctional treatment program. *Journal of Offender Counseling, Services and Rehabilitation,* 7: 5-22, 1982.

18. Wilson, Deborah G.: *Persistent Felony Offenders in Kentucky: A Profile of the Institutional Population.* Louisville, Kentucky Criminal Justice Statistical Analysis Center, 1985.

19. Wolfgang, Marvin E., Figlio, Robert M., Tracy, Paul E., and Singer, Simon I.: *The National Survey of Crime Severity.* Washington, D.C., U.S. Government Printing Office, 1985.

20. Wright, Kevin N., Clear, Todd R., and Dickson, Peter: Universal applicability of probation risk-assessment instruments: A critique. *Criminology* 22: 113-134, 1984.

CHAPTER ELEVEN

EVALUATION RESEARCH
IN CRIMINAL JUSTICE

T HIS CHAPTER introduces the fundamentals of evaluation research, also known as program evaluation. As we shall soon discover, evaluation research is more of a research purpose than a research
method.[2] Indeed, evaluation research usually involves a wide variety of
research techniques. Since evaluations generally take place in action settings, they bring forth a whole set of unique problems and constraints.
These will be discussed later in the chapter.

In recent years, evaluation research has taken on a new importance.
The proliferation of federal programs and the requirement that these
programs be evaluated have created new interest in this type of research.
In addition, researchers have begun to view evaluation research as an
important specialty area. There is also new concern over the impact of
policy and program changes. Evaluation research can help to make decisions when resources are scarce and choices must be made between competing programs.

PURPOSE OF EVALUATION RESEARCH

Evaluation research serves many useful functions. The three most
common uses include providing information for: (1) rational decision-
making, (2) feedback and monitoring of program performance, and (3)
assessment of program impact.

In today's complex world of decision-making, criminal justice administrators and managers must have accurate, concise, and timely information to make well-informed decisions. For example, are one officer
patrol cars more cost-effective than two? Do they provide less safety for

the officers? Do they improve response time? These are the types of questions facing decision-makers. Information from evaluation research can help provide some answers. It is important to remember though, that evaluation research will not replace decision-making, it will only aid it.

A second major function of this type of research is to provide feedback and monitoring information to permit program modification, improvement, reduction, or reallocation of resources. Many evaluation designs permit on-going information feedback concerning performance. For example, a probation department which uses intensive supervision may want information to determine whether or not a high level of contacts and services are being provided to the probationers consistently over time. They may also find that certain types of treatment modalities are more effective than others. Providing this type of information on a regular basis allows the program decision-makers to make changes and adaptations as necessary. Indeed, it is only after careful review and consideration that a program should be abolished.

Perhaps the most widely used purpose of evaluation research is to assess program performance and impact. This effort involves determining to what degree a program has met its stated objectives. It may also involve determining the impact a program has as a result of having met its objectives. For example, a neighborhood crime watch program may have as one of its objectives a reduction in the number of certain types of crimes. It may even meet these objectives, however, the overall impact of this program may mean that crime is simply being displaced into other neighborhoods. This discovery may in turn lead to the development of a new crime prevention strategy. The point is, evaluation research can be an effective tool for measuring program impact and outcomes, some of which may be difficult to discover or anticipate. Of course, this type of information is also helpful for researchers attempting to better understand crime and its patterns and effects.

Before we discuss the fundamentals of evaluation research it is important that the constraints and problems associated with this endeavor be discussed.

CONDUCTING EVALUATION RESEARCH

Unfortunately, evaluation research in criminal justice, as well as other human service areas, is beset with a number of constraints which directly impinge upon, and frequently reduce the usefulness of the generated information. Ideally, evaluation research should be made an on-going part of the agency or program. This would greatly reduce the con-straints imposed on the evaluator. However, given the realities of the criminal justice system, the researcher must be prepared to deal with the limitations that often exist. The four major types of constraints which hamper criminal justice research include: measurement, political, ethi-cal, and data-net issues.

The first and perhaps the most problematic of the constraints is the difficulty of measuring concepts. On the one hand lies an issue inherent in translating frequently vague program goals into measurable indica-tors of achievement. The program goals being measured must be crucial to the program objectives, not simply the easiest to study. Vaguely for-mulated program goals are more often the rule rather than the exception within social programs, especially in the pre-1970 period of criminal jus-tice. While such ambiguous goal statements as "reducing recidivism," "preventing delinquency" and "enhancing the socioeconomic environ-ment of parolees" may serve useful purposes for action programs in re-ceiving support and funding from different and potentially conflicting interest groups within the criminal justice system, such statements are essentially useless for evaluators confronted with the problem of devel-oping appropriate indicators for measuring the attainment of these goals. In order for goals to be measured, they must be stated in concrete and concise terms. For example, a delinquency prevention program might want to reduce the percentage of dropouts from school, or the number of runaways, or increase the number of youth involved in extra-curricular activities. These are all measurable objectives that might have an impact on the amount of delinquent behavior that occurs.

In addition, Glaser[9] has identified another reason for "goal displace-ment" — the fact that several levels of program goals often exist. Glaser identifies two levels of goals: manifest and latent. Manifest, or "official" goals are proclaimed in the legislation, directives, or formal announce-ments under which programs are created. It is here that universal goals, such as "reducing crime" are often developed. Latent goals are those that reflect the actual day-to-day procedures and practices of the program.[31] For example, the manifest goal of a halfway house may be to "reduce crime," but its programs may be based on providing treatment for of-fenders with a drug problem. Curing drug abuse would be an example of a latent goal. One example of this problem can be found in an evalua-tion of a crime suppression program conducted by Vito, Longmire, and Kenney.[30] During the initial stages of the research, they were surprised to find that the program objectives were stated in a rigorous and measurable manner. For example, the formally stated objectives included:

1. Decrease the number of reported burglaries by 10 percent.
2. Increase by 20 percent the number of arrests for the seven major index offenses over that of the previous year.

Despite these well formulated objectives, questions remained. What was the basis for such statements of expectations and were they realistic? Upon investigating further, they found that the program officials had literally copied their objectives from the examples given by the funding agency's request for proposals. The program officials assumed that in order to receive the funds they needed to state their objectives in a percentage format. This was not the intent of the funding agency. The end result of this practice can be an impediment, rather than an aid to rational planning in criminal justice. In order to be plausible, such objectives must have a basis in fact, and they should be representative of the desired goals of the program. Vito, Longmire, and Kenney concluded that, "If the objectives are stated in a quantifiable fashion, but do not reflect the operations of the program, they can serve no purpose with regard to planning. If the evaluation is conducted on this basis, the result will be a smokescreen or whitewash."

Evaluation research, for the most part, involves reducing complex behaviors, attitudes, and interdependencies into simple models of causation or outcomes. It is not sufficient, as has often been attempted in the past, to infer program relationships without attempting to measure or control intervening and interrelated variables. As Weiss[25] has suggested, the evaluator is faced with "the task of sifting the real from the unreal, the important from the unimportant, perhaps even uncovering the covert goals that genuinely set the direction of the program but are unlikely to surface in open discussion." Part of the difficulty lies in operationalizing the goals of the program. As defined by Skogan,[19] operationalization "is the translation of concepts being measured into terms workable in light of the measurement technology to be employed." Three of the more common, and most difficult concepts to measure in criminal justice are recidivism, clearance rates, and justice (due process of law). Each of these will be discussed in some detail.

Recidivism

Recidivism is the most familiar impact measure. It is most often used to evaluate the effectiveness of rehabilitation programs. It is one measure which everyone takes for granted and the meaning of which is accepted by the public without question. Wilkins[26] notes that recidivism "simply means that the offender, once treated-punished, has offended again and that the subsequent offense has been placed on his record." Unfortunately, it is the simplicity of this definition which has lulled people to sleep:

> What has been done to offenders, and particularly to those offenders variously labeled recidivists, has been assumed to be the direct outcome of **their** actions—in a simple cause-effect relationship. This has enabled the false logic to be accepted that the behavior of the recidivist provides sufficient definitions and that it has not been necessary to look any further into the defining process.

Recidivism is typically operationalized as an offender who has committed a new crime as measured by a new arrest, conviction, or incarceration over a specified time period. In addition, it is possible for an offender to be considered a recidivist without committing a new crime but for failure to maintain the conditions of probation or parole—a "technical violator." The choice of one of the indicators of recidivism will have a definite impact upon the resultant outcome.

To test this proposition, Hoffman and Stone-Meierhoffer[10] drew a 50 percent sample of federal prisoners (N = 1806) serving a maximum term of more than one year and a day, who were released during the first six months of 1970 and then measured their recidivism rates with different indicators. The authors found that, during their first year of release, 29 percent of the prisoners had been arrested, 15.4 percent had been convicted, 12.6 percent had been sentenced to 60 days or more and 8.7 percent had been sentenced to prison. Thus, with the same group, the range of potential recidivism rates is extensive. It is also indicative of the manner in which the criminal justice system operates. Not all recidivists are even arrested, let alone convicted or incarcerated. Even though recidivism is a measure of failure, if one relies upon official records, it cannot include all of the offenders who commit a new crime. To make matters worse, there is a possibility that having a prior record can increase the probability of arrest and further cloud the issue of guilt.

The length of the follow-up period is also a crucial factor. With regard to recidivism, it has long been held that the longer the offender stays out of trouble with the law, the less likely they are to get into trouble with the law, and that recidivism should begin to be counted as soon as offenders have the opportunity to commit new offenses. For example, the President's Task Force on Corrections[17] cited previous studies on probation and parole outcome and concluded that they "reveal consistently that most difficulties with offenders occur within the first one or two years under supervision. For those who avoid difficulty through this period, the probability is exceedingly good that they will no longer be involved in criminal activity." This belief, plus the fact that the pressures of time upon the researcher often prevent lengthy follow-up periods, has led to the common adoption of a one year tracking period.

Yet, here again, Hoffman and Stone-Meierhoffer's research indicates that the length of the follow-up period can exert influence over recidivism rates. After six years, 60.4 percent of the aforementioned sample had been arrested, 41.7 percent had been convicted, 34.3 percent had been committed for 60 days or more and 27.5 percent had been sentenced to prison—rates which were all significantly higher than those calculated one year after release from prison.

From this overview, the student can see that there are a number of measurement problems concerning the use of recidivism as an outcome indicator. The choice of an operational definition of recidivism is often dependent upon the purpose of the study and the availability of data.

Clearance Rate by Arrest

The most common performance measure of police productivity is the clearance rate by arrest. Skolnick[20] has written that the clearance rate is considered the most important measure of accomplishment for detectives, and it was recommended as a control measure by Chief O. W. Wilson, one of the leading authorities on police management and professionalization.

The operational definition of the clearance rate is the percentage of crimes known to the police which the police believe have been solved by the arrest of the offender. It is important to note that the designation "cleared" is a police organizational term which bears no direct relation to the administration of the criminal law. In short, the clearance rate has nothing to do with the detection of guilt or the attainment of conviction. Also, since it is based upon offenses known to the police, the clearance rate is subject to all of the difficulties surrounding citizen reporting of crimes mentioned in our analysis of the UCR (see Chapter Four). It is also important to mention that the arrest of one person can clear several crimes or several persons may be arrested in the process of clearing one crime. Table 11.1 is a listing of national clearance rates for the 1984 crime index.[8]

The social process of clearing crimes also affects the validity of this

TABLE 11.1

CLEARANCE RATE BY ARREST FOR
1984 INDEX OFFENSES

Index Crime	*Clearance Rate by Arrest*
Murder and Non-negligent Homicide	74%
Aggravated Assault	61%
Forcible Rape	54%
Robbery	26%
Burglary	14%
Larceny-Theft	29%
Motor Vehicle Theft	15%

Source: Federal Bureau of Investigation, *Crime in the United States, Uniform Crime Reports* (Washington, D.C.: U.S. Department of Justice, 1981), p. 153.

measure. One problem relates to what Pepinsky[16] has termed the "policeman's dilemma":

> The irony is that although police are supposed to be hired and paid for preventing crime, their importance is likely to be seen as a measure of how many offenses they report or arrests they make.

As with any performance measure, the police may feel pressured to represent themselves in the best possible light and may manipulate rates accordingly. For example, Skolnick[20] lists three commonalities which the police can offer in return for the defendant's cooperation in the clearance process: (1) reduction of charges and counts, (2) concealment of actual criminality, and (3) freedom from further investigation of prior offenses. After all, the defendant who "cops out" also "clears" himself since he is afforded virtual immunity from future arrests on past crimes. Thus, a well-motivated attempt to develop a performance standard can undermine due process of law. A similar example would be the prosecutor who claims a 90 plus percent conviction rate, but neglects to mention that the vast majority of cases plead guilty.

The criminal justice evaluator who wishes to gauge the efficiency of police performance must be aware of the process surrounding the calculation of clearance rates and attempt to develop some independent measure of efficiency.

Justice

A final example of the measurement problem involves the concept

TABLE 11.2

PROBABILITY OF RECEIVING THE DEATH PENALTY
IN FLORIDA, GEORGIA, TEXAS, AND OHIO:
BY RACE OF OFFENDER AND VICTIM

Offender/Victim Racial Combinations	Overall Probability of Death Sentence			
	Florida	Georgia	Texas	Ohio
Blacks kill white	.221	.167	.087	.254
Whites kill white	.046	.042	.015	.046
Blacks kill black	.006	.005	.001	.017
Whites kill black	.000	.028	.007	.000

Source: Bowers, William J. and Glenn L. Pierce, "Arbitrariness and Discrimination Under Post-*Furman* Capital Statutes," *Crime and Delinquency* (1980), p. 594.

"justice." Kobrin[11] has forcefully argued that justice should be considered as an outcome of criminal justice programs and policies.

> Agents of criminal justice assume, perhaps uneasily that improved effectiveness in the control of crime follows improved efficiency in the use of their sanction resources, just as day follows night. In this investigation of this naive theory, evaluators find themselves obliged to accept program input variables at face value, dutifully assessing their ultimate impact on crime rates.

There is no doubt that due process of law (often defined as "equality of justice"), should be considered as a proper research focus.

Yet, justice, as one might expect, is often difficult to operationally define. The most common benchmark is that of the Fourteenth Amendment itself—equal justice under the law, that all persons should be treated by the law with the same consideration.

A recent example of this type of research is a study of the administration of the death penalty in four states (Florida, Georgia, Texas, and Ohio) following the guidelines established by the *Furman* decision by Bowers and Pierce.[4] Their research question was essentially one of due process: Had the post-*Furman* statutes eliminated the arbitrary and discriminatory application of the death penalty? The authors examined the interaction between the race of the victim and the race of the offender in order to determine if persons sentenced under constitutionally acceptable death penalty statutes were equally likely to receive capital punishment. The results of their analysis in Table 11.2 reveals that there were stark differences by race of both offender and victim in all four states. Black killers and the killers of whites were substantially more likely than others to receive a death sentence. The authors controlled for the effect of several variables and examined different stages of the criminal process and the general pattern still held. They concluded that "the burden of proof should now be shouldered by those who argue that the death penalty can be imposed without arbitrariness and discrimination."

As Levine and his associates have indicated,[14] "It is easier to define injustice than to prove it." Even in this particular study, it is difficult if not impossible to discern exactly where the pattern of arbitrariness and discrimination originates. Yet, it is important that the researcher make the attempt to determine if due process is being followed. Indeed, it may be the most important outcome variable which can be considered.

As we can see from the above examples, defining, operationalizing and measuring the concepts and variables associated with criminal justice can be a difficult and time-consuming process. Unfortunately, there are additional problems which plague the evaluator in criminal justice.

A second problem that researchers should be aware of is the political nature of social programs. As Weiss[14] has indicated, many programs are "political creatures" which have emerged from political bargaining. Accordingly, the performance of these programs is occasionally attached to the reputations of sponsors, careers of administrators, jobs of staff members, and expectations of the clientele. In addition, organization investment via budgetary interests (appropriations for future funding) may adhere to the continued existence of programs. New and innovative programs in criminal justice are particularly fraught with political considerations.

Ensuing pressures for a positive evaluation may place the researcher in a precarious position. Involving the administrator and program staff early in an evaluation effort are tactics to reduce much of the friction (as well as facilitate sharper focuses on and definition of operational definitions, ease of access to data, and establishing definitions of expectations by all parties). Indeed, without the support and cooperation of the program administrators and staff, a successful evaluation is nearly impossible. Unfortunately, it is the new and innovative program that is given the most scrutiny, while older, more established programs frequently escape evaluation. The result of this practice is that we often continue to spend large amounts of money on programs and policies of which we know little about their true effectiveness.

A major aspect of the political arena concerns the posture of the program administrator vis-a-vis the researcher. Twain[22] has indicated that for these participants, the rewards provided by the research study are markedly different and are ultimately related to their status. Typically, researchers are members of a profession in which status and advancement depend upon productivity in ways which have more to do with their ability to develop information about the research approach than with the success or failure of a particular program. Accordingly, a researcher may be willing and often eager to criticize program assumptions, but reluctant to question the implemented research techniques. On the other hand, the career of the administrator is tied to the performance of the program. Campbell[5] has suggested that one solution to this problem would be for the administrator to adopt an "experimental" stance, pragmatic, forward-looking and more interested in finding solutions to problems than in justifying a particular choice of a solution. It is clear that some negotiation is in order, with the interests of each party clearly defined. The researcher must demonstrate the value of his project in terms of its relevance for social and agency problems.

It is also important to note that often a slow but definite process of cooptation occurs in which the researcher associates closely with the program under study. This may be the result of financial needs, friendship, or desire for future research opportunities. In any event, it is important that the researcher maintain an objective and unbiased view. One suggestion is to have colleagues review the research and offer criticisms and suggestions.

Evaluation results are many times considered an "all or nothing" proposition, magnifying the pressures and constraints on a research effort. There may be, of course, situations in which a program should be abandoned, but only after considerable evaluation and thought. If evaluations are conducted properly, they should provide information for monitoring, adjusting, and improving a program. Only after considerable attempts of this type have been made should a program be dismantled.[29]

A third problem concerns ethical issues inherent in superimposing an experimental research design which would include assignment of clients into experimental and control groups. This problem is encountered in almost all areas of social research and is not endemic only to the field of criminal justice; the use of random assignment is currently expressly forbidden by Federal guidelines for research[15] and previously was not a frequent achievement. As Adams[1] states, "the most frequent objection to random assignment is made on such ethical and legal grounds that it is improper to deny or withhold presumably beneficial treatment from eligible subjects simply through their assignment to a control group." (See Chapters Three and Four.) Accordingly, researchers commonly utilize a number of quasi-experimental techniques through which the program is evaluated by means of information from the treatment group and a comparison group chosen in a manner which makes the latter similar to the treatment group in those characteristics believed to be related to performance. An example of this type of design was utilized by Vito[28] in his study of a drug and alcohol program called "Papillon." The comparison group was constructed by following a procedure in which inmates who were not admitted to the program due to "non-prejudicial" reason, such as men who were paroled early, or entered alternative programs. The assumption was that this "self-drop" group was comparable to the experimental group. (See Chapter Six.)

Despite the fact that the quasi-experimental design has the potential to yield more accurate results, there is considerable evidence which indicates that evaluation research in criminal justice has largely ignored this procedure, although recently this has begun to change.

The final major obstacle facing the researcher in the area of criminal justice is what we will refer to as a data-net problem, or the condition of the information system itself. This problem is due in large part to legal constraints and "bureaucratic inertia," in which the researcher is often frustrated in initial attempts to obtain information from the criminal justice system.

Program record and agency files are sources of evaluation data. Programs usually collect a fairly large amount of information about what they do and the subjects they deal with. Unfortunately, experience has suggested that organizational records are not as useful as they could be. Both the organization's record keeping, and the transfer of intake and service information to permanent records tends to be haphazard. Records may be missing, inaccurate, unverified, out-of-date, and incomplete. This problem is acute when a researcher attempts to gather information on recidivism. Indeed, there is evidence that a great deal of variation exists between "official" data and the actual number of crimes committed.[12,27] Police files simply do not provide an accurate or complete record. Furthermore, program definitions and categories are seldom created for evaluative purposes. Vital categories of information may never have been requested, or records may be kept in a form (such as narrative case-recording) that reduction to items which are usable for evaluation research may be difficult to interpret.[24] Most of these problems can be solved by beginning the research **with** the program, not as an afterthought. The research results are generally more dependable when the research is built into the program, rather than superimposed on top of it.

In addition to the problem of obtaining data in usable form, the accessibility problem can be severe. Many records, especially those related to recidivism, are maintained within different administrative units. To have a complete record, a researcher might be required to access several criminal justice agencies. Receiving permission to view these records is often difficult, at best. For example, one way to track the criminal record of an offender is through a "RAP" sheet, but since many police departments and particularly the Federal Bureau of Investigation, as departmental policies, do not provide information for research purposes it is difficult to obtain this information. Even when agency data are coupled with available F.B.I. data, there will be numerous cases of nonagreement, contradiction and missing information. In view of these constraints, evaluators are forced to define their outcome measures in less than ideal terms and to operate with incomplete data. There has been some success with self-reporting techniques[6,12] (see Chapter Four) however, it is not always possible to locate offenders, and the cost may be prohibitive.

Overall, the quality of evaluation research in criminal justice must be viewed in terms of these constraints. An awareness of these problems, coupled with thorough preplanning can help minimize these obstacles.

THE PROCESS OF EVALUATION

As defined by Rossi and Wright,[18] evaluation research is "any scientifically based activity undertaken to assess the operation and impact of public policies and the action of programs introduced to implement these policies." The primary purpose of evaluation research is the determination of the extent to which a program achieves its goals, and the assessment of whether that success was actually a function of the program activity.

Evaluation of social programs essentially involves four basic steps:[21]

1. Setting the objectives
2. Measuring the objectives
3. Determining the degree of success
4. Making recommendations

Although the above steps tend to focus on the controlled experiment[13] and thus have a limited utility, they do represent the basic logic to most evaluative efforts.

The first step involves formulation of the program's objectives. Usually this is done by the program and its staff, however, as mentioned previously, often the stated goals are too broad and vague. The role of the researcher in this case is to work with the program staff and administration to arrive at some mutually agreed upon objectives. The key is to develop measurable objectives.

This brings us to the next step; the identification of the proper criteria to be used in measuring the programs success or impact. What this step entails is the determination of indicators of performance. For example, if one of the programs goals is to reduce the fear of crime among the elderly in a certain area, we might develop a questionnaire addressing issues related to the fear of crime. If a reduction in the recidivism rate among probationers is a goal, we might operationally define recidivism as the further engagement in criminal activities. Our indicators might include the number and type of arrests, convictions, technical violations, and the severity of the criminal activity.

The determination and explanation of the degree of success is just that. It involves designing an appropriate research design, gathering data, translating it into usable information, and attempting to explain the degrees and reasons for success and failure. It is once again important to mention that evaluation research should not be seen as an all or nothing proposition. Rather, it should be viewed as a tool to help programs become more effective and efficient.

Finally, the researcher should make recommendations for future program activity. These might include expansion of the program, or modifications in the program's operation. Perhaps the program is having limited success with alcoholic offenders. The recommendation may be to use more community resources, or to hire an alcoholic treatment specialist. Recommendations are designed to give some direction to the program staff and administrators on how to improve the program and its operation.

MODELS OF EVALUATION RESEARCH

Although most evaluation research efforts involve several conceptual models used in conjunction, we shall discuss several of the more popular models used in criminal justice individually.

As defined by Washington,[23] the goal-attainment model stems from a conception of evaluation as the measurement of the degree of success or failure encountered by a program in reaching predetermined goals. A basic premise of this model is that if the ultimate goal were met, then a series of prior accomplishments would have been fulfilled. This model emphasizes the measurement of outcomes rather than inputs, assuming that, if the goal were met, then the appropriate combination of inputs would have been made. Analytically, measuring goal attainment involves five steps. They are as follows:

1. Specification of the goal to be measured.
2. Specification of the sequential set of performance that, if observed, would indicate that the goal had been met.
3. Identifying which performances are critical to the achievement of the goal.
4. Describing the "indicator behavior" of each performance episode.
5. Collectively testing whether each "indicator behavior" is associated with each other.

One limitation of the goal-attainment model centers around the fact that evaluators often ignore the function between ends and means, or output and input.

A second model of evaluation research is called the impact model. A major assumption of this model is that in order for the evaluator to estimate the effects of a particular program, it is necessary to compare the experiences of the recipients of services or treatment with those of some reference group, or comparison group. The question raised by this model is "What difference does the intervention make?" In this sense, the impact model is more rigorous than the goal-attainment model. It assumes that, in order to determine what differences the intervention makes, it is necessary to measure the relationship between the program goals (the dependent variables) and a variety of independent variables, including the personal characteristics of participants, the program components, and the conditions under which the program operates. If, for example, you were attempting to determine whether or not drug counseling had an effect on drug users, you would develop a comparison group of drug users that did not receive drug treatment and compare them on a number of outcome indicators, such as recidivism, continued drug use, or employment. You would also attempt to distinguish whether or not certain characteristics were related to success or failure, such as age, sex, marital status, or prior convictions. You would also look at whether there were varying levels of treatment within the groups and whether or not this had an effect.

The third model we shall discuss is the cost-benefit or cost-effectiveness model. This model is closely associated with systems analysis, and could be classified as part of a systems model of evaluation since it focuses upon rational choice decisions from among competing alternatives. Although many view cost-benefit analysis as an alternative to evaluation research, it is really a logical part of the evaluation process.[28] Washington in discussing the assumptions and usage of cost-benefit analysis, defined the technique in the following manner:

> Cost-benefit analysis involves the use of economic theories and concepts. It is designed to tell us why a program or one of its components works in addition to how well it works. The concept of cost-benefit defines the relationship between the resources required (costs) to attain certain goals and the benefits derived. One of its basic premises is that many decisions involving the allocation of limited resources are often made on the basis of how those resources can be most optimally used, avoiding waste, duplication, and inefficiency. Cost-benefit analysis is a tool for decision makers who need to make choices among viable competing programs designed to achieve certain goals. It is not designed to favor the "cheapest" nor the "costliest" program, but rather the optimal program in terms of the available resources and the explicit goals.

The cost-benefit model is not without its limitations. It is a very difficult and time consuming procedure that has a heavy reliance upon certain assumptions. It is also very difficult, if not impossible to measure "social" costs and benefits. This is particularly true with regard to criminal justice. For example, while the costs of competing correctional alternatives such as prison, halfway houses, and probation may be determined, the "social" costs are more difficult to gauge. What are the effects on one's family if you're incarcerated, and what about the costs to the victim if you commit another crime while on probation? We simply cannot put a price upon the costs of violent crime, or the subsequent fear of crime that results. Likewise, we do not know what benefits might have accrued if probation was used instead of a prison term. Because of these problems, cost-benefit analysis has not been widely used in criminal justice research.

TYPES OF EVALUATION DESIGNS

The three basic types of evaluation research methods in criminal justice are the non-experimental, the quasi-experimental, and the experimental.

Although each of these designs are discussed in detail in Chapter 6, we shall briefly examine their application to evaluation research.

The non-experimental evaluations include a wide variety of research methods. Those most common to criminal justice include the case study, before-after, survey, and time series designs, and cohort analysis. It also appears that the non-experimental designs are the most popular in criminal justice. The reasons for this vary, but generally it is because they can be applied to poorly understood problems, they can allow more in-depth information (such as in a case study), they are generally cheaper and faster, and they may pose less of a threat to staff and administrators.

There are also many problems associated with these methods. The information may be biased, reliability can be suspect, the results may not have much generalizability, and as in the case of surveys, the information is out-dated quickly. There is also a problem when non-experimental designs are used to measure treatment effects. Without comparison group figures on recidivism, our crime rate reductions have very little meaning. Despite these drawbacks, non-experimental designs remain popular in criminal justice.

Quasi-experimental methods usually include making use of a treatment group and a comparison group that is selected because it is similar to the treatment group. Cases are not randomly assigned, but rather gathered from files that resemble, at least roughly the treatment group. Quasi-experimental designs are used primarily because random assignment is usually not permissible, particularly when treatment is withheld that could be beneficial. Quasi-experimental designs are also useful in complex operations where assignment to groups randomly is impossible in a way that would insure comparability. In this instance, quasi-experimental designs may be superior to random assignment. There may also be natural experiments where quasi-experimental designs are useful because they can be developed quickly, or because there simply are no random cases available. For example, the Gideon Decision[7] resulted in the release of 1,252 Florida inmates. The Florida Department of Corrections wanted to know the possible effects of such a release. They compared 110 of the early releases to a matched comparison group of 110 full-term releases. After a 28-month follow-up, the early releases showed a 13.6 percent recidivism rate compared to a 25.4 percent rate for the full-term cases. The use of an experimental design would have been impossible under these conditions, but through the use of a quasi-experimental design, the Florida correctional officials were able to determine that the early release of offenders into the community did not trigger a "crime wave" as some had predicted.

Although there is some evidence that quasi-experimental designs are as accurate as experimental designs, particularly in criminal justice settings, the fact is that many evaluations are conducted without even the benefit of this type of design. The end result is that we are often left with research that tells us little about the true effectiveness of a program since there is no basis for comparison.

The controlled experiment is the researcher's favorite type of design, but it is also the least found in criminal justice research. The experimental design involves random assignment to either a treatment group or a control group. Treatment or stimulus is then administered to the experimental group and the effects are measured and compared to the control group.

Controlled experiments are not as prevalent as they once were. Many of the reasons have already been offered, and it appears that quasi-experimental designs are increasingly replacing the once sacred experimental design.

CITIZEN CRIME PREVENTION: AN EXAMPLE OF AN EVALUATION

In recent years it has become popular for neighborhoods to form neighborhood crime watch projects. These projects are designed to increase public awareness about crime and to provide neighborhood "crime watchers" to patrol or observe the neighborhood. The following is an example of an evaluation of one rather unique program.

In July 1977, the city of Columbus, Ohio implemented the Citizen's Crime Reporting Project (CCRP), a project based on the general deterrence model.[13] The primary objective of the program was to determine whether citizen involvement and participation could significantly reduce crime and perceived victimization in a high crime area.

This program differed from other similar programs in several respects: (1) citizen patrollers were paid minimum wages; (2) formal training was conducted by the police academy; (3) patrollers were in constant contact with police via the CCRP coordinator; (4) the full-time administration implemented and reinforced rules and guidelines; and (5) both in-house and external evaluations were performed.

Since, as with most social programs this project had multiple objectives, no single measure of program performance was sufficient to evaluate the project's impacts on the community. Thus, several performance indicators were developed. Measure of program effectiveness included:

1. The proportional reduction (or increase) in selected crime in the project area, and for a similar time frame in the previous year.
2. The proportional reduction (or increase) in selected crime in the project area and contiguous areas as compared to similar time frame in the previous year.
3. The attitudes of project area residents regarding the effectiveness of the project and its potential impact on the police, the community, and crime.
4. The attitudes of the police officers responsible for the project area regarding the effectiveness of the program and its potential impact on the police, the community, and crime.

Data were available from the police department for the year preceding the project (pre-experimental) and during the project's operation. Similarly, telephone interviews were made prior to the inception of the program and during the eighth and twelfth month of the program. Selected crime data were also gathered and compared to a control area to discover whether displacement ("spillover") of criminal activity from the project area to surrounding areas was occurring. In addition, the activity logs of the patrollers were reviewed as were the general operations of the program.

It should be mentioned that the multiple objectives of this program posed certain problems in determining project impact. On one hand, the project sought to increase citizen-police cooperation and thereby encourage the reporting of crime. On the other hand, it sought to reduce crime as reflected in crimes "known to the police." Obviously, to achieve one objective might frustrate the other, therefore, multiple measures were included in this evaluation.

Table 11.3 presents data on type I offenses for the treatment area and comparison precinct areas (census tracts 12 and 13), and the entire city.

With the exception of grand larceny (up 20 percent), every category or reported crime dropped for the treatment area. In the cases of rape and aggravated assault, the small number of incidents prevents generalizations. Within the project area, burglary and auto theft clearly decreased. The declines in the reported numbers of burglary and auto theft are particularly important because these categories contain offenses which are most likely to be deterred by the presence of citizen

TABLE 11.3

CRIMES KNOWN TO THE POLICE
IN THE TREATMENT AND COMPARISON AREAS

Comparison Areas	AREAS			
CRIME	Treatment Area (%)	Fourth Precinct (%)	Ninth Precinct (%)	City (%)
Rape	− 6	− 4	− 4	− 4
Robbery	− 19	− 17	+ 2	− 7
Aggravated Assault	− 34	+ 3	+ 7	+ 9
Burglary	− 10	− 2	+ 9	+ 2
Grand Larceny	+ 20	− 2	+ 21	− 7
Larceny	− 3	+ 5	− 16	− 14
Auto Theft	− 2	+ 21	+ 15	+ 14

Source: Latessa, Edward J. and Allen, Harry E. "Using Citizens to Prevent Crime: An Example of Deterrence and Community Involvement," *Journal of Police Science and Administration* (March, 1980) pp. 69-74.

TABLE 11.4

CITIZEN ATTITUDE SURVEY

STATEMENTS	Pretest		April		October	
	N	%	N	%	N	%
CCRP will interfere with the police in crime prevention:						
Agree	23	9.1*	9	10.0*	1	1.1*
Disagree	231	90.9*	81	90.0*	90	98.9*
CCRP will be a success						
Agree	238	93.3	80	87.9	82	92.1
Disagree	17	6.7	11	12.1	7	7.9
I like the police						
Agree	193	77.5	66	77.6	106	89.8
Disagree	56	22.5	19	22.4	12	10.2

*Significant at the .05 level.

Source: Latessa, Edward J. and Allen, Harry E. "Using Citizens to Prevent Crime: An Example of Deterrence and Community Involvement," *Journal of Police Science and Administration* (March, 1980) pp. 69-74.

TABLE 11.5

ATTITUDES OF POLICE TOWARD PROJECT-SELECTED QUESTIONS

STATEMENTS	April		December		September	
	N	%	N	%	N	%
This is a dangerous neighbor-hood:						
Agree	60	82.2	28	93.3	25	92.6
Disagree	13	17.8	2	6.7	2	7.4
CCRP will be helpful in prevent-ing crime						
Agree	18	25.0*	14	46.7*	18	66.7*
Disagree	54	75.0*	16	53.3*	9	33.3*
CCRP will interfere with crime prevention						
Agree	59	83.1*	14	48.3*	7	25.0*
Disagree	12	16.9*	15	51.7*	20	75.0*
CCRP will be a success						
Agree	14	19.7*	7	25.0*	13	48.1*
Disagree	57	80.3*	21	75.0*	14	51.9*

*Statistically significant at the .05 level.

Source: Latessa, Edward J. and Allen, Harry E. "Using Citizens to Prevent Crime: An Example of De-terrence and Community Involvement," *Journal of Police Science and Administration* (March, 1980) pp. 69-74.

crime patrols.[3] The data pertaining to spillover indicated that there was an increase in auto thefts in precinct four, but the data did not indicate any clear evidence of crime being displaced into areas contiguous to the treatment census tracts.

The next area examined was citizen attitudes. Community attitudes toward the project were deemed critical, since the program was based on citizen involvement in crime prevention. The citizen responses are presented in Table 11.4. The attitudinal data revealed that while there were some shifts, the citizens presented a positive view of the project from the beginning.

A final objective of the evaluation was to determine police attitudes toward the project. It was hypothesized that strong negative attitudes of police toward CCRP would hinder police/project cooperation and reduce project effectiveness. The data in Table 11.5 reveals a marked change in police attitudes, from a relatively negative stance before the inception of CCRP to one of universal tolerance after implementation began. It is reasonable to suggest that police attitudes toward CCRP improved. Indeed, it might even be possible that the officers' beliefs that the CCRP patrollers would be a hindrance rather than a help were proven to be unfounded.

Among the recommendations made included continuation of the project, and possible expansion into other high crime neighborhoods.

The above example illustrates the fundamentals of evaluation research. This evaluation was done with minimum disruption to the program and its staff, and at a relatively low cost. Although this program was not without its problems, the information provided by the evaluation allowed the administrators and staff to better gauge the progress they had made, and it also provided their funding source with performance data upon which they could make more informed decisions about the program's future.

EVALUATION RESEARCH STAFF

One of the critical questions facing decision-makers is that of who will conduct the research. Adams identified several possibilities:[1] in-house staff also called internal evaluators, university faculty, private for-profit research firms and private non-profit research firms, all called external evaluators. Choosing which is best depends in large part on the agency, the program under study and the resources available. Most large police departments and departments of correction have internal research staffs, while smaller agencies cannot afford, nor do they require permanent research staff. Naturally, there are some issues surrounding both internal and external evaluators. The internal research unit is more familiar with the agency and its objectives. They have ready access to information, communication with administrators is facilitated, and they can quickly respond to the agencies' needs. On the other hand, they may not be as qualified, and their results are more open to criticism because of their relationship to the organization. External evaluators may have more expertise, but will need to spend more time acquainting themselves with the program and agency. External evaluators, particularly university faculty, may be more interested in basic research and may be less willing to provide decision-making information in the form of recommendations. There have been cases where university faculty "grab the data and run," concerned more with publishing the results and criticizing the program than with providing useful information. However, for the most part external evaluators can provide the agency with objective results without investing in permanent research staff.

CONCLUSION

This chapter has reviewed the basics of evaluation research, which is rapidly becoming the most widely used form of research in criminal justice. Evaluation research can be described as applied research. Research that is designed to provide information concerning the operations, effectiveness, and impact of a program. It occurs in action settings and, while there are a number of constraints associated with it, most can be overcome through an awareness of the problems and adequate planning.

The models and research methods employed by evaluators varies widely, ranging from non-experimental case studies to cost-benefit analysis. Most evaluations employ several methods and techniques.

Evaluation research is best suited for "action" settings. It is designed to provide criminal justice decision-makers with reliable information upon which to make programmatic decisions. As with all research processes it is fraught with pitfalls and problems, most of which can be overcome through pre-planning and awareness of the environment.

KEY TERMS

Data net
Cost-benefit analysis
Impact model
Goal-attainment model
Multiple performance indicators
Internal evaluator
External evaluator

STUDY GUIDE

1. What are the primary purposes of evaluation research?
2. How can evaluations aid decision-makers?
3. What are the four most common constraints imposed upon evaluations?

4. Discuss the various models of evaluation research and how various components can be used simultaneously?
5. Who conducted evaluation in criminal justice?
6. Name some of the indicators of "recidivism." How might you measure them and what are the possible sources of information?
7. What are "latent" objectives? "Manifest" objectives?
8. What are some of the problems associated with "clearance rates by arrest"?
9. Define "justice." How would you operationalize this concept?
10. Why is a 12-month follow-up of offenders insufficient?

REFERENCES

1. Adams, Stuart: *Evaluation Research in Corrections.* Washington, D.C.: U.S. Department of Justice, 1975, pp. 66-73.
2. Babbie, Earl: *The Practice of Social Research.* Belmont, Wadsworth, 1983.
3. Bickman, Leonard, et al.: *Citizen Crime Reporting Projects' National Evaluation Program: Phase I Summary Report.* Washington, D.C., U.S. Department of Justice, 1977.
4. Bowers, William J. and Glenn L. Pierce: Arbitrariness and discrimination under post-*Furman capital statutes. Crime and Delinquency, 4:* 563-635, 1980.
5. Campbell, Donald: Reforms as Experiments. In Caporaso, James A., and Leslie L. Roses (Eds.): *Quasi-Experimental Approaches.* Evanston, Northwestern University Press, 1973, p. 224.
6. Clark, John and L. Tifts: Polygraph and interview validation of self reported deviant behavior, *American Sociological Review. 31:* 1966.
7. Eichman, Charles: *Impact of the Gideon Decision Upon Crime and Sentencing in Florida: A Study of Recidivism and Sociocultural Change.* Tallahassee, Florida Division of Corrections, Research Monograph No. 2, December 1965.
8. Federal Bureau of Investigation: *Crime in the United States, Uniform Crime Reports 1984.* Washington, D.C., 1985, p. 152.
9. Glaser, Daniel: *Routinizing Evaluation: Getting Feedback on Effectiveness of Crime and Delinquency Programs.* Rockville, National Institute of Mental Health, 1973, p. 22.
10. Hoffman, Peter B. and Barbara Stone-Meierhoffer: Reporting recidivism rates: The criterion and follow-up issues. *Journal of Criminal Justice, 8:* 53-60, 1980.
11. Kobrin, Solomon: Outcome variables in program evaluation: Crime control, social control, and justice. In Klien, Malcolm W., and Katherine S. Teilmann (Eds.): *Handbook of Criminal Justice Evaluation,* Beverly Hills, Sage, 1980: pp. 447-458.
12. Krohn, Marvin, Gordon Waldo, and Theordore Chiricos: Self reported delinquency: A comparison of structured interviews and self-administered checklists. *Journal of Criminal Law and Criminology, 65:* 545-553, 1975.
13. Latessa, Edward J. and Harry E. Allen: Using citizens to prevent crime: An ex-

ample of deterrence and community involvement. *Journal of Police Science and Administration, 8:* 69-75, 1980.

14. Levine, James P., Michael C. Musheno, and Dennis J. Palumbo: *Criminal Justice: A Public Policy Approach.* New York, Harcourt, Brace and Jovanovich, 1980, 523-524.

15. National Commission for the Protection of Human Subjects of Biomedical and Behavioral Research: *Protection of Human Subjects.* Washington, D.C., Department of Health, Education, and Welfare, 1977, pp. 3077-3078.

16. Pepinsky, Harold E.: *Crime Control Strategies: An Introduction to the Study of Crime.* New York, Oxford Press, 1980, pp. 104, 247.

17. The President's Commission on Law Enforcement and Administration of Justice: *Task Force Report: Corrections,* Washington, D.C., U.S. Government Printing Office, 1967, pp. 320.

18. Rossi, Peter H. and Wright, Sonia R.: Evaluation research: An assessment of theory, practice, and politics. *Evaluation Quarterly, 1:* 5-52, 1977.

19. Skogan, Wesley G.: *Issues in the Measurement of Victimization.* Washington, D.C., U.S. Government Printing Office, 1981, p. 7.

20. Skolnick, Jerome: *Justice Without Trail: Law Enforcement in Democratic Society.* New York, John Wiley & Sons, 1975, pp. 164-175.

21. Suchman, Edward: *Evaluation Research.* New York, Sage, 1967, p. 28.

22. Twain, David: Developing and Implementing A Research Strategy. In Struening, Elmer, and Marcia Guttentag (Eds.): *Handbook of Evaluation Research.* Beverly Hills, Sage, 1975, pp. 27-52.

23. Washington, R.O.: *Program Evaluation in the Human Services.* Milwaukee, Center for Advanced Studies in Human Services, 1977, pp. 20-26.

24. Weiss, Carol: *Evaluation Research.* Englewood Cliffs, NJ, Prentice-Hall, 1972, pp. 72-73.

25. Weiss, Carol: Evaluation Research in the Political Context. In Struening, Elmer, and Marcia Guttentag (Eds.): *Handbook of Evaluation Research.* Beverly Hills, Sage, 1975, pp. 13-26.

26. Wilkins, Leslie T.: *Evaluation of Penal Measures,* New York, Random House, 1969, pp. 43-44.

27. Williams, Jay R. and Martin Gold: From delinquent behavior to applied delinquency. *Social Problems, 20:* 209-229, 1972.

28. Vito, Gennaro F.: Does it work? Problems in the evaluation of a correctional treatment program. *Journal of Offender Counseling, Services and Rehabilitation, 7:* 5-21, 1983.

29. Vito, Gennaro F.: Shock Probation in Ohio: A Comparison of Attributes and Outcome. Unpublished doctoral dissertation. Columbus, Ohio State University, 1978, pp. 68-73.

30. Vito, Gennaro F., Dennis R. Longmire, and John P. Kenney: Cracking down on crime: Issues in the evaluation of crime suppression programs. *Journal of Police Science and Administration, 11:* 38-41, 1983.

31. Vito, Gennaro F. and Deborah G. Wilson: *The American Juvenile Justice System.* Beverly Hills, Sage, 1985, pp. 109-121.

INDEX

209

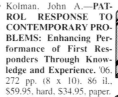
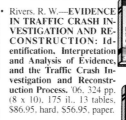
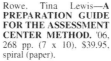

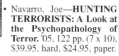
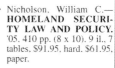

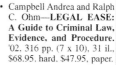